THE NIGHT BEFORE COOKBOOK

THE
NIGHT BEFORE
Cookbook

Paul Rubinstein
&
Leslie Rubinstein

Illustrations by Shelly Sacks

THE MACMILLAN COMPANY · NEW YORK
COLLIER-MACMILLAN LTD · LONDON

The Macmillan Company, New York
Collier-Macmillan Canada Ltd., Toronto, Ontario

Printed in the United States of America

To Margot

CONTENTS

FOREWORD

Paul Rubinstein is the only man I know whose fondest wish is a duck press for Christmas. The only person I've ever met who would prefer polishing his copper pots to spending Sunday mornings in bed. And the only husband I've ever heard of who actually dreams of soufflés, popovers, and moules marinières.

Paul was not only born with a silver spoon in his mouth—it was filled with pâté de foie gras. From his earliest childhood he has colorful memories of gastronomic delights—of expeditions, en famille, to a river to fish and the subsequent 24-hour preparation, by every member of the household, of the day's catch; of a six-hour drive along bumpy French roads with his father to a particular restaurant for a particular saddle of hare luncheon; of the joys of learning to cook an omelette at an age so tender that the rest of us were barely comprehending hopscotch.

As a schoolboy he managed to trade his ordinary cheese sandwiches for the beluga caviar-filled goodies of a friend. ("Tell your cook," he would confide to the son of a movie mogul, "to keep giving you sandwiches of that strange black stuff.") And, in the Army, so I've been told, he was so distressed over the quality of Uncle Sam's cuisine that he bet the cook twenty dollars that a Rubinstein-prepared roast beef would far outdraw the beef prepared in the usual way. The result? Not only twenty dollars but the life-long awe of the cook, who cheerfully did his best to arrange gourmet meals for the young wizard chef—even to the extent of having Alaskan King Crabs flown in specially and putting thick sirloins at Paul's squad's disposal, while the rest of the battalion obliviously munched on ordinary Army grub.

To say that Paul is an unusual cook is an understatement. I think you will sense that upon close inspection of this book.

First of all, Paul is an uncompromising purist. Therefore he has not minced words about the necessity of the finest quality products, their absolute freshness, and the necessary equipment for the ultimate in culinary excellence.

THE NIGHT BEFORE COOKBOOK is not for constant weight-watchers or budget-fretters. Butter *is* butter—and what an experience when it's correctly used! Inferior cuts of meat are just that, and no doctoring under the sun can fool the discerning palate. Neither is this book for those cooks who want to impress guests with exotically named dishes, hastily prepared—a simple stew, lovingly made and without a fancy title, can be utterly delicious. That is Paul's credo. And we hope you will enthusiastically agree.

What role does the wife-of-the-chef play? In this case she observed her aproned husband for countless hours in the kitchen and acted as Chief Chopper, Washer, Chairman in Charge of Tearing Lettuce, General Assistant, and Number Two Taster. Ah, the hours spent shopping for the "right" fresh horseradish root, "the" perfect oyster sauce from an out-of-the-way shop in Chinatown, "the" most aromatic herb, "the" ideal coffee bean, "the" best imported dried mushroom. And the scrubbing of mussels, the shaving of chocolate, the shelling of peas!

I have sat, mesmerized, as Paul happily made stock and watched his pot brew. I have observed him patiently staring through the glass oven door as his freshly baked bread was rising. I have seen him create a beautiful sauce with the grace and ease of Fred Astaire. And approach a supremely satisfying repast with the same excitement some people feel about a Rembrandt, a World Series homer, a political victory.

THE NIGHT BEFORE COOKBOOK has been an adventure to prepare. Our work is done. Now it is time for you to get a taste of the fun.

LESLIE RUBINSTEIN

INTRODUCTION

The purpose of this book is to offer a solution to a problem that is rapidly becoming more acute. The problem is a result of two opposing trends, each tending to create difficulties for the other.

On the one hand, we are in the midst of a great awakening to the subtleties and pleasures of fine cooking and fine food. Travelers in ever increasing numbers return from abroad to find the usual fare at the local supermarket or grocery inadequate. They want more sophisticated foods; they seek unusual ingredients. The markets and the food processors are responding—and the result is a fantastic array of exciting foods that would have gathered dust on the shelves 15 years ago, but which now can scarcely be kept in stock.

On the other hand, there is a tremendous change in the demands on the time of single women, wives, and mothers. The care of children too young for school takes constant attention, but this is only one of the many distractions from cooking. Millions of women have full time jobs. Others have heavy schedules of participation in community events, local politics, the arts, and adult education. All of these activities seem to create one problem: *not enough time to cook.*

One answer is to rely on the numerous prepared and packaged foods that require only minutes to "heat and serve." But this is not satisfactory to the creative hostess. There is no feeling of accomplishment in "heat and serve" cooking, and you always run the risk that your guests have the same package of the same frozen preparation at home. They can tell the difference, just as you can when you are served a mass-produced meal.

The solution offered here makes several assumptions. It assumes that when you invite people to dinner, you want to serve them something special, something that demonstrates your ability in the kitchen, and something that they couldn't have found in a restaurant too easily. It assumes that you are willing to make the effort to achieve a desired effect. It assumes that you are not looking for shortcuts, and that you do not skimp on calories or grocery money when guests are coming or when you're preparing for a special family occasion. Our answer to the time problem is a collection of recipes that can be prepared, in large part, *the night before*.

We have set one arbitrary standard for these recipes: that they require no more than 60 minutes preparation just before serving. (Most require much less time—or none—at the zero hour.) Everything else can be prepared in advance.

The advantages of using recipes planned this way are many. The pressure is off, and you don't have to work with your ear cocked for the sound of the doorbell. It stands to reason that if you are dressed to receive guests, you are not dressed for cooking, especially if you're preparing something that might splatter or stain. By using these recipes, you take advantage of your kitchen privacy on the night before. Even the best and most experienced cooks make mistakes—but the night before you still have time for repairs or even substitutions if disaster strikes! You can indulge your artistic bent for decorating food, which requires a certain leisure. If your kitchen is not large, you will find it's quite a blessing to have the cumbersome pots used, washed, and put away before your last-minute preparations even start, and before you need space for clearing the dishes away from the table. Best of all, you can serve dishes you never believed you could do because you never had the time.

Now a brief review on what you will—and won't—find in the following pages. The first chapter suggests the appliances and equipment you should have for best results in your kitchen. Then come the recipes, from hors d'oeuvres to desserts, and finally 20 suggested menu combinations, planned to offer taste contrasts and balance. Each recipe is divided into two parts, one indicating everything to be done the night before, and the other giving the last few steps just before serving. Most of the recipes serve six people, precise numbers are given in every case. (Some recipes, such as salad dressings and beverages, give the liquid yield rather than number of servings.) Pay close attention to the instructions for overnight storage care—they can make the difference between success and failure!

We have not attempted to follow any particular pattern of national origins in these recipes. In addition to American dishes, you will find recipes from China, Italy, Japan, Polynesia, France, Russia, Spain, Greece, England, Persia, Germany, Mexico, Ireland, Norway, North Africa, Hungary, Brazil, Poland, Austria, and Switzerland. Also, the recipes cover the whole spectrum of time and difficulty, ranging from the very simple and quick to the time-consuming and somewhat complicated. All they share are excellence and the fact that they can be partly pre-prepared.

You won't find any diet dishes here, nor was any particular attention paid to budgeting. We advise against substituting margarine for butter, but some substitutions of ingredients are suggested when there is a danger that a particular item might not be available. Maximum use of fresh ingredients—vegetables, herbs, fruits, meats, and eggs—is recommended. If you must substitute a vegetable or a fruit that is out of season or unavailable, use a "fresh-frozen" one rather than a canned one. With herbs, the most important thing to remember is that dried herbs produce a much stronger flavor than fresh, so you must compensate in quantity. And no prepared baking mixes allowed!

Each recipe begins with a complete list of the ingredients necessary. Where no precise quantity is given, you need far less than the smallest amount you can buy. We avoid the expression "season to taste" because if you have never tasted a particular dish, you cannot know how to season it. We advise strongly that you follow the seasoning measurements exactly the first time you prepare any dish. Then if you detect a seasoning that doesn't suit your taste, note it on the recipe for future adjustment.

You will note that in several of the recipes we recommend the use of Maggi's liquid seasoning. According to the label its ingredients are "Hydrolyzed Plant Proteins, Water, Salt." The effect of adding a *small* quantity of this seasoning liquid to a recipe is an enhancement of the flavors of the ingredients of that recipe without the intrusion of Maggi's own taste. Maggi's is not available at all groceries, but the only preparation that comes close to substituting for it is soy sauce (any brand), and even this is not the same thing. Our advice is to use Maggi's if you can find it, but not to worry if you can't.

A parting word of caution. Be sure to read every recipe—including the ingredients—through to the end before beginning work. Also check your utensils and your storage materials. It can be tragic to be lacking a vital herb or an essential pot when you're halfway through a recipe in the middle of *the night before*!

I

EQUIPMENT

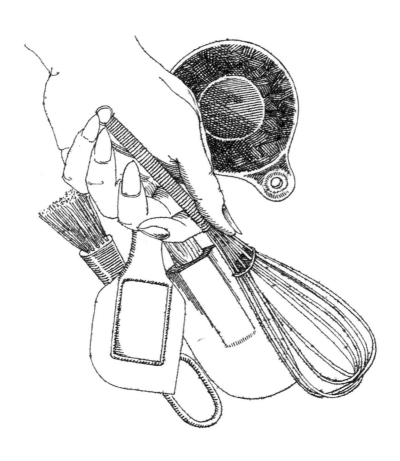

I

Lovers of food and cooking almost without exception are highly susceptible to the urge to buy kitchen equipment. Let loose in a well stocked hardware store or housewares department, they invariably go into a trance. Their glazed eyes reflect the glories displayed on the gadget rack, the hard brightness of the copper pots, the steely shine of those beautiful French knives. Naturally the knowing salesman descends at this moment, and the victim goes home with another often unnecessary and usually expensive acquisition for his kitchen.

We can't pretend to offer any cure for this ailment—we are afflicted with it ourselves. But what we have set forth here is a sober listing of what we consider *essentials* for the kitchen. These are not necessarily related to night before cooking—you would use them all the time. Definitely essential to night before cooking are the storage containers and materials we suggest, which should be kept on hand and in good quantity at all times.

APPLIANCES

Besides cooking equipment and accessories, kitchen appliances large and small have a strong appeal for a devoted chef. If you are in the fortunate position of being able to do anything about your major appliances—building a house, remodeling a kitchen, or even just replacing an appliance, for example—we hope our advised comments here will be of help.

Refrigerators. We might as well come right out with it: In our opinion a well equipped kitchen has two refrigerators. There is no such thing as enough refrigerator space. We became the proud possessors of a second refrigerator only recently, and of course, two are quite inadequate—we need three.

But assuming your kitchen has the normal quota of refrigerators —that is, one—night before cooking requires optimum use of the storage space you do have. Before you so much as chop an onion for your night before preparations, it is a good idea to clear the decks in your icebox by removing everything possible. Chances are many things on the shelves can be stored elsewhere. Unopened jams and jellies need not be ice cold. Potatoes keep very well in any cool dry place. Soda water and ginger ale are usually served over ice cubes—they don't need to be cold when poured. Many fruits taste better when they are not iced, and refrigeration arrests their ripening. The same goes for many cheeses, which really belong in an airtight cheese bell equipped with a moisture-retaining device. The only canned goods that truly belong in your refrigerator are the frozen ones; all the rest can go in a cupboard.

Stove. The electricity versus gas argument will probably never end, and each has its eloquent proponents. Naturally we feel compelled to say something on the subject. The one most important advantage of gas over electricity for cooking is control. Electric stoves may be cleaner, more automatic, less liable to break down, and possibly less expensive to operate in certain areas of the country. But if an omelette is beginning to burn a little, or a sauce that is supposed to simmer starts to boil, a flick of the wrist on a gas stove solves the problem, while the cook using electricity too often faces a ruined dish. Electric cooking does require much more skill and careful attention than gas.

The waist-high oven, by the way, is one of the best designs ever. If you're buying a new stove, get an oven with glass doors and a light inside!

There is one small piece of equipment that deserves special emphasis here: an oven thermometer. It is too seldom installed, yet it is absolutely vital to accurate cooking. Most kitchens·have a meat thermometer, some have a candy thermometer, but few have an oven thermometer. The temperature dial on your oven control can be off by as much as 100 degrees. Only an oven thermometer can tell you the exact temperature of the inside of your oven. You can hang one from an open rack or stand it up on its own little frame. Keep one in your oven at all times. An added precaution: Never wash the thermometer while it's hot, but remove it from the oven and wait until it reaches room temperature.

Blender. A good, two-speed blender is invaluable, preferably one with a jar that has a handle and a double lid (one small lid set inside the larger one). There are more sophisticated blenders on the market with many speeds and even with heating elements for cooking, but in our opinion these are expensive frills.

Mixers. We consider a good, heavy-duty mixer indispensable, and if it has meat grinder and juicer attachments, so much the better. We strongly recommend also having a small, portable mixer that you can use for small mixing jobs and for brief top-of-the-range stirring.

Other Small Appliances. Naturally every good kitchen has a serviceable toaster. Nice to have but not really necessary are electric knife sharpeners, can openers, juicers, ice crushers, and the like.

MANUALLY OPERATED COOKING EQUIPMENT

Here are the utensils you really need: A wall-mounted can opener, a food mill, several sizes of whisks, a cheese grater, a heavy-duty meat grinder with several blades, a kitchen scale (balance type), scissors, poultry shears, tongs, a rotary egg beater, and a selection of strainers. You also must have wooden spoons, small and large rubber scrapers, small and large spatulas, oven thermometers (one for each oven your stove may have), and candy, fat, and meat thermometers. A slotted spoon, measuring spoons and cups, a ladle, a grater, a two-tined fork, and several sizes of mixing bowls are indispensable. For baking you need a rolling pin, pastry board, pastry brushes, pastry bags with a selection of tips, circular dough cutters, a cake testing needle. And last but not least important are a potato masher, a funnel, a colander, a peeler, a complete set of good carbon steel knives, cutting and carving boards, a selection of molds, an ice pick, a melon baller, and a pepper mill.

POTS AND PANS

You can never have too many pots and pans, but you must have a kettle, several sizes of saucepans, several frying pans, a double boiler, a coffee pot, and a number of heavy enameled casseroles in several sizes, with lids. You also need a deep stock pot, roasting pans, pie pans, ovenproof glass baking dishes, soufflé dishes, bread pans, custard cups, a cookie sheet, a fish poacher, a crêpe pan, and (optional but very useful) a chafing dish. The chafing dish is especially desirable for night before cookery because it can combine the functions of reheating and serving right at the table.

STORAGE MATERIALS

Night before cooking requires you to have at hand, in a complete range of sizes, the square or rectangular semi-flexible plastic refrigerator containers with covers. You will be using them constantly, for everything from a small quantity of sauce to enough meat for a Stroganoff for 12 people. Also you should have a good collection of glass jars of different sizes with tight-fitting tops. For storing food in bowls or other open vessels, you will need lots of plastic film wrap. Freezer wrap is essential, and plenty of aluminum foil both wide and narrow, waxed paper, plastic sandwich bags, and paper towels. Heavy brown paper is most useful, as is a roll of good quality cheesecloth. It is a good idea also to have a roll of white paper tape to label your stored dishes. This saves you from the danger of pouring the chocolate into the beef stew!

INGREDIENTS

Among the staples you keep in your kitchen should be an ample selection of herbs and spices. Other important items are sugars— granulated, confectioners powdered, and both light and dark brown. Stock only the best olive oil for salad dressings, and several kinds of vinegar. (Some of the less expensive salad oils are all right for cooking, but please, only good olive oil in the dressings.) Red and white cooking wine should be available, as well as soy sauce, MSG (monosodium glutamate), Maggi liquid seasoning (our favorite), coarse kosher salt, both all-purpose and cake flour, and some brandy, Cointreau, and other liqueurs for flavoring.

II

HORS D'OEUVRES
AND APPETIZERS

II

AVOCADO-STUFFED TOMATOES

6 medium tomatoes (ripe but firm)
3 slices bacon
2 ripe avocados, peeled and pitted
2 tbsp. lemon juice
¼ cup finely chopped onion
3 tbsp. olive oil

¼ cup finely chopped green pepper
1 clove garlic, pressed or finely minced
¼ tsp. salt
⅛ tsp. pepper
3 anchovy filets, cut in half to make 6 pieces

NIGHT BEFORE:

1. Boil 2 qts. water in saucepan. Dip tomatoes in, one at a time; then peel them, slice off shallow cap from each, and scoop out seeds and pulp with melon baller. Refrigerate tomato shells.
2. Fry or broil bacon until crisp. Drain, then crumble into bits.
3. In mixing bowl, blend together avocados, bacon bits, lemon juice, chopped onion, olive oil, chopped pepper, garlic, salt, and pepper.
4. Refrigerate filling overnight in tightly covered bowl.

JUST BEFORE SERVING:

1. Fill tomato shells with avocado filling. There should be enough to fill tomatoes and protrude above tops.
2. Garnish each tomato with piece of anchovy on top and serve.

SERVES 6.

CAMEMBERT CHEESE DIP

1 8-oz. size Camembert cheese
(or similar soft ripe cheese)
1 cup sherry

⅓ cup unsalted butter
¼ cup finely ground white
almonds

NIGHT BEFORE:

1. Carefully remove white crust of cheese, retaining soft inside.
2. Place cheese in a bowl, add sherry, and let stand covered overnight in refrigerator.

JUST BEFORE SERVING:

1. Pour off remaining sherry. Soften butter.
2. Cream butter and ground almonds with cheese, turn into serving bowl, and chill in freezing compartment for ½ hour. Serve as dip with crackers or chips.

MAKES ABOUT 1½ CUPS.

CHICKEN LIVER PÂTÉ

½ lb. butter
1 lb. fresh chicken livers
¾ cup coarsely chopped onion
½ cup finely chopped celery
1½ cups chicken broth
½ tsp. paprika
½ tsp. salt

¼ tsp. pepper
1 clove garlic, crushed
½ cup cognac or brandy
1 envelope unflavored gelatin
1 cup chopped toasted almonds
2 hard-cooked eggs, chopped
coarsely

NIGHT BEFORE:

1. In heavy enameled saucepan, melt butter, add chicken livers, onion, and celery and sauté gently for about 10 minutes, or until livers are browned but pink in the center, and onions and celery softened.
2. Now add half the chicken broth to pan, and paprika, salt, pepper, and garlic. Simmer a few minutes, then remove from heat and add cognac.
3. In a separate saucepan, dissolve gelatin in rest of chicken broth.

Then slowly bring it to a simmer until all the grains disappear.
Turn off heat and let stand.

4. Now put chicken liver mixture into blender and run at high
speed until quite smooth. Transfer to mixing bowl, stir in gelatin stock, almonds, and hard-cooked eggs. Pour into 6-cup
mold and refrigerate overnight.

JUST BEFORE SERVING:

1. Dip mold into hot water for a few seconds, then reverse onto
serving platter.
2. Serve immediately with crackers or toast wedges.
    MAKES ENOUGH FOR 6-CUP MOLD.

CHINESE CH'UN CHUAN SPRING ROLLS
WITH PLUM SAUCE

These Spring Rolls are the delicious younger cousins of the ubiqui-
tous Egg Roll encountered at the top of almost every Chinese restaurant
menu. We first encountered them in a Shanghai-style restaurant. They're
not as difficult to prepare as might appear on first glance.

✒ *STUFFING*

½ *cup celery, minced*
1 *cup shredded cabbage*
2 *tbsp. soybean oil*
½ *cup cooked shrimp, diced*
½ *cup cooked meat, diced*
½ *cup water chestnuts (fresh
or canned), chopped*

½ *cup shredded bamboo shoots
(fresh or canned)*
2 *small onions, minced*
1 *tsp. salt*
½ *tsp. pepper*
¼ *cup soy sauce*

✒ *PANCAKES*

1 *lb. flour*
2 *tbsp. cornstarch*
1 *tsp. salt*
1 *large egg*

1 *tsp. sugar*
½ *cup soybean oil*
1 *egg white*

TO MAKE STUFFING:

1. Cook celery and cabbage in ½ cup water in saucepan until
tender. Drain.

2. Heat oil in frying pan. Add shrimp and meat to warm them. Add vegetables and seasoning.
3. Cook thoroughly. Allow to cool.

TO MAKE PANCAKES:

1. Sift together flour, cornstarch, and salt in large bowl.
2. Beat in egg and sugar. Add just enough water (about 1 qt.) to beat to a smooth, light batter.
3. Grease a 6" frying pan well with oil. Ladle ¼ cup batter into pan. Make pancake by tilting pan to spread batter evenly. Cook over low heat.
4. When pancake shrinks from edges of pan, carefully turn over.
5. Place cooked pancakes on plate and cool.
6. Place pancakes one at a time on board. Fill with 3 tbsp. stuffing, spreading neatly into oblong mold.
7. Fold one long side of pancake over stuffing. Then fold both short ends.
8. Brush remaining long side with egg white and seal.
9. Place stuffed pancakes in covered dish and refrigerate overnight.

JUST BEFORE SERVING:

1. Place oil 2" deep in 10" frying pan, or use deep-fryer. Heat.
2. Fry rolls until golden brown.
3. Drain on absorbent paper. Serve hot with Plum Sauce.

SERVES 6−8.

∾ *PLUM SAUCE*

12 ozs. plum jelly	*4 tsp. granulated sugar*
6 ozs. chutney, chopped fine	*5 tsp. vinegar*

Heat ingredients in saucepan. Blend evenly.

MAKES 2 CUPS.

CLAMS CASINO

36 *fresh cherrystone (or Little*   *Cracked pepper*
  Neck) clams   *1½ cups minced green peppers*
¾ cup tomato paste   *12 slices bacon, cut in thirds*
Maggi liquid seasoning (optional)

NIGHT BEFORE:

1. Scrub clams thoroughly. Open clams, discarding top shells. Arrange clams on broiler pans.
2. On each clam put ¼ tsp. tomato paste, a dash of Maggi, a pinch of cracked pepper, ½ tsp. minced green peppers, and ⅓ slice bacon.
3. Refrigerate overnight, covering pans with waxed paper.

JUST BEFORE SERVING:

1. Place pans of clams 3″ from flame or filament of broiler set for medium high. Ready to serve when bacon is crisp (but not burnt).
2. Serve, 6 to a portion, on a bed of rock salt as a first course. Or, serve on big platter as hors d'oeuvres, but make sure to provide cocktail napkins or small plates nearby.

S E R V E S   6 .

CHICK PEAS SPREAD OR DIP

1 lb. dried chick peas   *¼ tsp. pepper*
1 cup olive oil   *⅓ cup chopped black olives*
½ cup finely chopped onion   *½ cup sour cream (optional,*
1 tsp. salt   *for dip)*
2 tbsp. lemon juice

NIGHT BEFORE:

1. Wash and quickly parboil chick peas. Turn off heat and let them soak 1 hour.
2. Pour off water, cover with fresh cold water, and simmer over medium heat 2 hours.
3. Drain chick peas; then combine in a bowl with all other in-

gredients except sour cream, and mash until well mixed and smooth. (This can be done in a blender.)

4. Refrigerate overnight in covered container.

JUST BEFORE SERVING:

1. Spread on crisp crackers (thin wheat crackers are perfect) and serve as hors d'oeuvres.
2. Or, mix in sour cream and use as a dip.

MAKES ABOUT 4 CUPS.

CURRIED BEEF HORS D'OEUVRES

This recipe is perfectly adaptable to cooked lamb, pork, or veal.

½ cup soy sauce
1 cup olive oil
¼ cup vinegar
2 cups cooked beef, cut in
* julienne strips*
1 medium onion, sliced thinly

½ stalk celery, sliced thinly
1 tbsp. peppercorns (not
* ground)*
½ cup mayonnaise
1 tsp. curry powder
Pinch of dry mustard (optional)

NIGHT BEFORE:

1. Mix soy sauce, oil, and vinegar in a shallow mixing bowl.
2. Add strips of beef and stir around, making sure all the meat is in liquid.
3. Add sliced onion and celery; sprinkle with peppercorns.
4. Marinate overnight in refrigerator, stirring once or twice during this time.

JUST BEFORE SERVING:

1. Mix mayonnaise and curry powder together thoroughly. Add dry mustard if desired.
2. Remove meat from marinade and drain in a sieve. (Do not dry out on paper towels or other absorbent material.)
3. Toss meat in serving bowl with curried mayonnaise and serve.

NOTE: This curried beef may be served as one item of a dish of varied hors d'oeuvres, such as deviled eggs, cucumber slices, shrimps, anchovies, pickled beets, etc.; or as an individual hors d'oeuvre accompanied by small crackers or chips.

MAKES 2 CUPS.

FRESH LOBSTER PÂTÉ

1 lb. cooked lobster meat
¼ cup lemon juice
¼ tsp. fresh ground white
  pepper
⅛ tsp. paprika

⅛ tsp. salt
1 garlic clove, mashed through
  a garlic press
1 cup olive oil

NIGHT BEFORE:

1. Run lobster meat through the finest blade of a meat grinder twice.
2. Add lemon juice, seasonings, and garlic and blend thoroughly with a fork.
3. Now slowly dribble olive oil into mixture, mixing constantly until you have a smooth paste.
4. Pack into covered jar or crock and refrigerate overnight.

JUST BEFORE SERVING:

1. Remove to serving dish by dipping crock into hot water for a minute, working a knife around the sides to loosen, and inverting onto serving dish. Use as spread for toast rounds or crackers.
2. Or, pre-spread toast rounds and add a pinch of chopped parsley on top of each.

MAKES ABOUT 2 CUPS.

HAM AND CREAM CHEESE BALLS

6 *hard-boiled eggs, chopped*   1 *cup ground cooked ham*
8-oz. *bar of cream cheese*   *Pinch of paprika*
   (*softened at room temperature*) ½ *cup finely ground walnuts*
1 *tbsp. chopped chives*

NIGHT BEFORE:

1. Mix all ingredients except nuts with wooden spoon in deep mixing bowl until well blended and fairly smooth.
2. Now roll into balls, about the diameter of a quarter.
3. Drop balls, one at a time, into smaller bowl containing ground walnuts. Agitate bowl to make ball roll around and pick up a fine crust of nuts.
4. Remove each finished ball by spearing it with a toothpick. Place on serving platter and refrigerate overnight, covered with waxed paper.

JUST BEFORE SERVING:

Merely remove platter from refrigerator—the ham and cheese balls are ready.

MAKES 40 BALLS.

GNOCCHI TIDBITS

1½ *tsp. salt*   1½ *cups freshly grated*
2 *cups cornmeal*   *Parmesan cheese*
1½ *sticks* (⅜ *lb.*) *butter*

NIGHT BEFORE:

1. Bring 4 cups water and salt to a boil in heavy saucepan. Add cornmeal a little at a time, stirring constantly, until mixture is smooth and pasty. Remove from flame, and place pan in larger flat pan of hot water.
2. Stir in I stick (¼ lb.) butter and I cup Parmesan until thoroughly blended.

3. Pour dough into shallow rectangular buttered pan, cover with waxed paper, and refrigerate overnight.

JUST BEFORE SERVING:

1. Cut meal into 1″ squares. Roll each square in remaining grated Parmesan and arrange in buttered baking dish, overlapping squares. Melt remaining ½ stick butter and pour over gnocchi. Bake in preheated 350° oven until brown (about 15 minutes).
2. Serve as pasta. Or, serve with toothpicks as hors d'oeuvres.

SERVES 6.

PICKLED ONIONS

3 dozen small white onions
½ cup olive oil
1 clove garlic (crushed)
1 cup apple cider
1 cup white wine
1 tsp. dry tarragon
1 tsp. powdered English mustard

1 tsp. black pepper (fresh ground)
1 clove
1 tsp. sugar
1 tbsp. chopped chives (if serving as condiment)

NIGHT BEFORE:

1. Drop onions into a saucepan of boiling water, turn off heat immediately, and after 1 minute, remove them from the water with a slotted spoon. Peel off outer skins.
2. Simmer onions in a combination of all ingredients except chives for about 10 minutes, or until tender but not falling apart.
3. Remove from heat and refrigerate overnight in the cooking liquid, covered.

JUST BEFORE SERVING:

1. Drain, stick with toothpicks, and arrange on platter (omit chives).
2. Or, serve as condiment, in a vegetable dish with some of liquid, sprinkled with chives.

QUICHE LORRAINE

This versatile pie makes an excellent appetizer or hors d'oeuvre when cut in very narrow wedges instead of full-size ones. It is also a perfect luncheon dish, served with a fresh salad. Here we offer several alternative fillings for the same crust.

◄§ *CRUST*

1½ cups sifted all-purpose flour	2 tbsp. vegetable shortening
6 tbsp. butter, cut into small	⅓ tsp. salt
pieces	½ tsp. sugar

◄§ *STANDARD BACON AND CHEESE FILLING*

6 thin strips bacon	¼ tsp. salt
2 tbsp. butter	¼ lb. French or Swiss Gruyère
4 egg yolks	cheese, cut in small cubes or
1½ cups heavy cream	grated
¼ tsp. Worcestershire sauce	

NIGHT BEFORE:

TO MAKE CRUST:

1. Sift flour into mixing bowl. Add all other ingredients.
2. Flake butter and shortening in flour with your fingers. This should be done quickly to prevent melting of fats. The bits of fat should be rolled around in the flour until they have the appearance of dry cereal flakes.
3. Now add 4 tbsp. cold water and blend it into dough, then gather dough into a ball.
4. Place ball of dough on floured surface. Blend fat with flour by pushing ball down with heel of hand, a little at a time, mashing dough flat and away from you for about 12″. When you have done this to all of dough, gather it together into a ball again, flour it, wrap in waxed paper, and put into freezing compartment of refrigerator 1 hour to chill thoroughly. If you want to prepare this dough even longer in advance, you can refrigerate it (not in freezing compartment) for several days.

5. While dough is chilling, butter inside of 9″ pie pan.
6. Roll out dough quickly on floured surface. Roll from center out to sides, turning dough occasionally to prevent its adhering to board. You should end up with a circle of dough 3″–4″ larger in diameter than your pie pan.
7. Preheat oven to 375°.
8. Turn dough into pie pan, trim edges, press down all around edge with folk, prick bottom at 1″ intervals with fork.
9. Weight down crust by placing second, smaller pie pan (buttered on the *outside*) on top of dough—this prevents bubbles from rising.
10. Bake 10 minutes. Remove from oven, remove second pie pan, prick bottom of crust again with fork, return to oven for a couple of minutes more until just barely beginning to color. Remove partially cooked shell from oven and store in cool dry place (do not refrigerate) overnight.

JUST BEFORE SERVING:

TO MAKE FILLING:
1. Preheat oven to 375°.
2. Blanch bacon strips in boiling water 3 minutes.
3. Fry bacon strips in butter until just turning brown, remove from heat, drain on paper towels.
4. Place egg yolks in mixing bowl and beat with electric beater or whisk. Slowly add cream, continuing to beat until thick and yellow. Add Worcestershire sauce and salt.

TO MAKE QUICHE:
1. Place layer of cheese cubes on bottom of partially cooked shell. Lay strips of cooked bacon over cheese. Pour cream mixture over top, leaving about ½″ space for puffing up.
2. Bake 30 minutes and serve immediately.

NOTE: You can also freeze the completed quiche (wrapping entire pie pan in foil). To serve, let it thaw out for 2–3 hours, bake again at 375° for 15–20 minutes until piping hot.

SERVES 6.

◄§ HAM AND CHEESE FILLING
Same as standard filling except replace bacon strips with julienne strips or cubes of boiled ham, (about ½ cup) mixed with cheese cubes.

◄§ CHEESE FILLING
Same as standard filling except replace the bacon with ham (as above) and replace the Gruyère cheese with equal amount (¼ lb.) of Blue Cheese, Roquefort, or Camembert, blended with 1 tbsp. chopped fresh chives.

◄§ SHELLFISH FILLING
Same as standard filling except replace bacon with the following, prepared as indicated:

1 cup cooked shrimp, crab, or   ¼ cup finely chopped onion
    lobster meat (or combination)   2 tbsp. butter

1. Sauté onion in butter until transparent.
2. Add shellfish and sauté 3–4 minutes more.
3. Place shellfish-and-onion mixture in layer over cheese in the pie shell.

NOTE: The variety of quiche fillings is limited only by your imagination. Once you have sampled the recipes given here, you can substitute other meats, fish, cheeses, and add vegetables (stewed tomatoes, squash, peppers, etc.) and garnishes (herbs, anchovies, etc.), as your fancy dictates.

ROLLED SANDWICH HORS D'OEUVRES

1 loaf unsliced white (or soft   ½ lb. paper-thin sliced prosciutto
    whole wheat) bread   (ham, paper-thin salami, corned
1 8-oz. package cream cheese,   beef, paper-thin smoked turkey,
    softened to room temperature   or smoked salmon may be sub-
Green food coloring (optional)   stituted)
1 bunch watercress   Fresh pepper in a mill

NIGHT BEFORE:

1. Trim crusts from loaf of bread, making sure to keep corners square.

2. Cut into very thin slices (about 20).
3. If desired, mash cream cheese with a few drops of green food coloring for a decorative effect.
4. Spread each slice of bread with thin layer of cream cheese, thin layer of watercress leaves, then thin layer of meat.
5. Grind a little pepper over the meat.
6. Roll slices carefully into little cylinders. If moistness of ingredients does not hold the shape, secure with a toothpick. Another way is to have a tray prepared; as you roll each sandwich, place it on the tray with open seam face down so that weight of sandwich keeps it pressed down. When tray is full, put a plastic place mat face down over the sandwiches, then a plastic film wrap tightly over the whole thing.
7. Refrigerate covered tray of sandwiches overnight.

JUST BEFORE SERVING:
Remove sandwiches to serving tray.
MAKES ABOUT 20.

RUMAKI
Polynesian Hors d'Oeuvres

12 chicken livers (very fresh)   12 water chestnuts
1 cup soy sauce   1 cup brown sugar
½ tsp. paprika   12 slices bacon
2 cloves

NIGHT BEFORE:
1. Marinate livers overnight in a mixture of soy sauce, paprika, and cloves, covered, in refrigerator.
2. Prepare other ingredients: halve water chestnuts and slices of bacon, and have toothpicks handy.

JUST BEFORE SERVING:
1. Preheat oven to 400°.
2. Remove livers from marinade, drain, and cut each liver in half.
3. Slit each half-liver, and insert a half-chestnut in the slit, then

dip in brown sugar, wrap half-slice of bacon around, and secure with toothpick.

4. Arrange the rumaki on cookie sheet or jelly roll pan, and bake for 20 minutes until crisp, turning over once.
5. Serve hot, or for buffet, in chafing dish over simmering water.

MAKES 24.

SASHIMI
Japanese Raw Fish Appetizer

The first reaction of most people to the idea of eating raw fish is one of disgust. But the Japanese people are famous for their cleanliness, and secondly for their intelligent and well-balanced diet. Since the Japanese are islanders surrounded by an abundance of fish, it is quite plausible that they've perfected a way to serve fish without cooking it at all. Sashimi can be prepared in very small quantities for the hesitant to try. We recommend garnishing it with horseradish, but a very strong mustard is good too. The traditional Japanese garnish is a very strong green horseradish powder, mixed with a little water into a stiff paste, and served in small (½ tsp.) dabs alongside the fish. This powder can be obtained in *some* Oriental specialty stores.

2 *lbs.* very *fresh pompano or*   ¼ *tsp. white pepper*
  lemon sole, or fresh tuna   1 *tsp. salt*
2 *cups lemon juice (fresh is best)* ⅓ *cup freshly grated horseradish*
½ *cup soy sauce*   6 *lemon wedges*
½ *cup very finely chopped*
  onions

NIGHT BEFORE:

1. Remove skin and bones from fish.
2. Mix all remaining ingredients except horseradish in a glass dish with a cover.
3. Immerse fish in marinade in covered dish overnight in refrigerator.

JUST BEFORE SERVING:

1. With a very sharp knife cut the fish into slices not less than ⅛" and not more than ¼" thick.

2. Arrange them either on serving platter or individual plates. With each portion serve a small dab of fresh grated horseradish and a wedge of lemon.

SERVES 6.

STUFFED SOFT ROLLS

1 *dozen small soft rolls*	¼ *cup milk*
1 *cup minced cooked ham*	½ *cup finely chopped onion*
1 *cup freshly grated sharp*	¼ *cup melted butter*
Cheddar cheese	*Paprika*

NIGHT BEFORE:

1. Split rolls lengthwise with serrated knife. Scoop out soft dough, leaving 24 shells. (Reserve the dough.)
2. In mixing bowl, blend minced ham and grated cheese.
3. Boil milk, turn off heat, immediately throw in soft dough and mix.
4. Now mix dough with ham and cheese mixture. Mix in onion.
5. Refrigerate mixture overnight, and store roll shells in a tightly covered container.

JUST BEFORE SERVING:

1. Preheat oven to 300°.
2. Fill shells with ham and cheese mixture, brush tops with melted butter, and sprinkle paprika over the tops. Arrange on a cookie sheet or flat baking pan, and bake about 20 minutes, or until cheese is just melting.
3. Serve hot.

MAKES 24 HORS D'OEUVRES.

III

SOUPS

III

COLD AVOCADO SOUP

2 large ripe avocados
2 cans jellied madrilene
2 tbsp. lemon juice
½ tsp. salt
¼ tsp. white pepper

1 tbsp. very finely chopped
onion
2 dashes Tabasco sauce
¼ tsp. Worcestershire sauce
½ pint sour cream

NIGHT BEFORE:

1. Pit and peel avocados.
2. Place in blender jar with all other ingredients except sour cream, and blend at high speed until well combined.
3. Leave in blender jar and refrigerate overnight, covered.

JUST BEFORE SERVING:

1. Put jar on blender, and blend again.
2. Serve in individual portions topped with generous spoonful of sour cream on each portion of soup.

SERVES 6.

GAZPACHO

Gazpacho can truly be called one of the beauties of Spain. In the south, almost every little Spanish village claims to be the birthplace of Gazpacho, and one does detect slight differences in flavor here and there. The soup is more than a soup: it is a salad, it is a vegetable dish; it can be elegant and festive or simple and earthy.

◄§ SOUP

1 cucumber	2 tbsp. olive oil
1 medium onion	½ tsp. paprika
1 clove garlic	¼ cup tomato juice (or V-8)
4 ripe tomatoes	½ cup cold water
1 green pepper	¼ tsp. salt
1 3-inch piece of celery stalk	⅛ tsp. white pepper

◄§ GARNISHES

1 cucumber, peeled and chopped fine	1 small onion, chopped
1 hard boiled egg, chopped	¾ cup small dry croutons
	1 small green pepper, chopped

NIGHT BEFORE:

1. To make soup: Peel and cut cucumber in chunks; peel onion and clove of garlic. Quarter tomatoes; scoop seeds out of pepper and cut it in chunks. Cut celery in small slices. Now pass all soup ingredients through blender, making a smooth liquid. (You may have to divide ingredients into 2 batches if you have a small blender jar.) Put soup in serving tureen.
2. Prepare garnishes as indicated, and place each in its own small serving dish (a set of custard cups is ideal).
3. Refrigerate everything overnight, in covered containers.

JUST BEFORE SERVING:

1. Stir soup thoroughly and ladle into serving plates.
2. Sprinkle a little of each garnish on surface of each plate of soup.

SERVES 6.

GREEK LEMON SOUP

6 cups chicken broth	¼ cup lemon juice
¼ cup uncooked rice	1 lemon, sliced thinly
2 tsp. salt	2 hard-boiled eggs, sliced thinly
3 eggs	(optional, for decoration only)

NIGHT BEFORE:

1. Combine broth, rice, and salt in large saucepan. Bring to boil. Reduce heat, cover, and simmer 15 minutes, or until rice is tender.
2. Remove from heat.
3. Beat eggs vigorously. Add lemon juice. Slowly add 2 cups of hot chicken stock. Whisk well.
4. Combine with remaining stock. Whisk until slightly thickened.
5. Cool to room temperature. Refrigerate overnight, covered.

JUST BEFORE SERVING:

1. Stir well.
2. Garnish with lemon slices and egg slices if desired and serve immediately.

SERVES 6.

ICED TOMATO SOUP

4 lbs. ripe tomatoes
2 tbsp. granulated sugar
4 tsp. salt
1 tbsp. onion juice
The juice of 1 lemon
Grated rind of 1 lemon

1 cup heavy cream
8 thin slices cooked ham, diced
½ cucumber, peeled and diced
4 dashes Maggi liquid seasoning
   (optional)
Finely chopped fresh parsley

NIGHT BEFORE:

1. In blender, purée tomatoes.
2. Pass through fine sieve.
3. Refrigerate in covered container overnight.

JUST BEFORE SERVING:

1. To tomato purée, add sugar, salt, onion juice, lemon juice, and lemon rind. Beat until smooth.
2. Stir in cream, add ham and cucumber. Add Maggi. Stir.
3. Garnish with parsley and serve immediately.

SERVES 6-8.

MADRILENE SURPRISE

3 *medium-sized tomatoes*
6 *cups clear beef stock (or*
consommé)
2 *stalks celery, cut in 1" pieces*
1 *medium-sized onion, peeled*
and quartered
1 *tsp. salt*

½ *tsp. black pepper*
2 *envelopes unflavored gelatin*
8 *fluid ozs. red caviar*
½ *pt. sour cream*
6 *tsp. chopped fresh chives*
6 *lemon wedges*

NIGHT BEFORE:

1. In covered saucepan simmer tomatoes in 1 cup beef stock for approximately 30 minutes. Tomatoes should be soft but still whole.
2. With a long fork, carefully remove tomatoes, one by one, and peel off skins with a sharp paring knife.
3. Force tomatoes through a fine sieve into a large saucepan filled with the other 5 cups stock. Add celery, onion, salt, and pepper.
4. Simmer over medium heat for 15 minutes.
5. Strain the liquid to remove onion and celery. For a perfectly clear consommé, use cheesecloth to remove every tomato seed. Cool.
6. Dissolve gelatin in ½ cup of the cool consommé. Add this mixture to soup and bring almost to a boil.
7. Refrigerate but do not let soup jell.
8. Place 2 heaping tbsp. caviar in bottom of each consommé cup. Fill cups ¾ full with the cooled consommé.
9. Refrigerate overnight, covered.

JUST BEFORE SERVING:

1. Place heaping tablespoon of sour cream in center of soup in each cup. Do *not* stir.
2. Sprinkle 1 tsp. chives over each mound of sour cream.
3. Serve with lemon wedge on each saucer.

NOTE: A variation of this soup can be prepared with either beef or chicken consommé (*no* tomatoes) and pressed or beluga caviar. The "surprise" is lost, but the taste is excellent.

S E R V E S   6 .

VICHYSSOISE

This soup may be served hot or cold.

3 *large leeks*   ½ *tsp. salt*
4 *medium potatoes*   ¼ *cup heavy cream*
2 *tbsp. butter*   6 *tsp. chopped fresh chives*

NIGHT BEFORE:

1. Wash leeks, cut off green tops. Slice paper-thin. Peel potatoes and cut into very small cubes.
2. In a 5- or 6-qt. saucepan cook leeks uncovered in 1 tbsp. butter for 5 minutes. Do not allow them to brown. Add potatoes and leave another minute. Now add 2 qts. boiling water and salt, and simmer slowly 40 minutes, skimming any scum that forms off the top.
3. Remove from heat, cover and refrigerate overnight.

JUST BEFORE SERVING:

Cold: 1. Remove from refrigerator, stir in cream.
          2. Pour into soup cups, sprinkle surface with chopped chives, and serve.
Hot: 1. Heat soup in a double boiler over simmering water for about 10 minutes.
          2. Stir in cream and heat another 5 minutes or so until heated through without boiling. Stir in remaining butter.
          3. Bring to table in tureen with chopped chives separate. Sprinkle 1 tsp. chives over each soup dish after serving soup.

S E R V E S   6 .

ARTICHOKE SOUP

3 *artichokes*   1 *tsp. Maggi liquid seasoning*
3 *cups chicken broth*   *(optional)*
1 *lemon, sliced thin*   ¼ *tsp. salt*
¼ *cup finely minced onions*   ¼ *tsp. white pepper*
                                    ½ *pint heavy (whipping) cream*

NIGHT BEFORE:

1. Wash artichokes thoroughly and drain to remove as much water as possible.
2. Cook artichokes over medium heat in broth for about 45 minutes, with lemon slices.
3. Remove artichokes from broth; reserve broth. Discard lemon.
4. Carefully remove artichoke bottoms and set aside. Now scrape pulp from ends of leaves and return pulp to broth.
5. Refrigerate overnight: soup in covered container, bottoms separately.

JUST BEFORE SERVING:

1. Heat soup to a simmer. Cut artichoke bottoms into cubes and add to soup.
2. Stir in onions, Maggi, salt, and pepper.
3. Whip cream until soft peaks are formed.
4. Stir whipped cream into hot soup, leave over fire for just a minute more, then serve immediately.

S E R V E S   6 .

BONGO BONGO SOUP
Purée of Oyster Soup

If you have any friends who are reluctant to try oysters, here is a lovely way to introduce them. In fact, you could even conceal the fact that there are oysters in the soup until after they've told you how good it is! We first tasted this soup at one of the Trader Vic's restaurants, put the head waiter through the third degree to get an idea of how it was made, and tried it at home the next day. This recipe is the result of much experimenting.

1 qt. fresh shelled oysters	⅛ lb. butter
1 pt. clam juice	2 tsp. salt
3 cans concentrated pea soup	1 tsp. pepper
½ cup white wine	1 pt. heavy cream

NIGHT BEFORE:

1. In saucepan, simmer fresh oysters with their own liquid, clam juice, and purée of peas over low heat for 15 minutes.

2. Stir in wine, butter, salt, and pepper.
3. Transfer soup into a blender, and blend at high speed until oysters are completely puréed. (You may have to blend in 2 batches because of amount of liquid.)
4. Return soup to saucepan. Cover and refrigerate overnight.

JUST BEFORE SERVING:

1. Reheat and stir.
2. Beat heavy cream until stiff.
3. Turn your broiler up to high. After filling each soup plate with soup, add a generous heaping spoonful of whipped cream. Do *not* stir.
4. Slide plate under broiler for a few seconds, until center of cream becomes toasted dark brown. Serve immediately.

NOTE: If oysters are unavailable, fresh clams or fresh mussels can be substituted.

SERVES 6.

CHEESE SOUP

1½ tbsp. butter
¼ cup sliced green onions
  with tops
1½ tbsp. flour
1½ cups milk
1½ cups chicken broth
2 raw carrots, peeled and cut
  into ¼" cubes
1½ cups (approx. ⅓ lb.)

shredded cheese: mild-to-
medium sharp natural cheeses
such as Cheddar, Gouda, Jack,
or Danish Dambo
½ tsp. salt
¼ tsp. paprika
⅛ tsp. pepper
2 tbsp. freshly chopped parsley
Paprika for garnish

NIGHT BEFORE:

1. Melt butter in a large saucepan. Add onions and sauté until they are limp.
2. Stir in flour, blending to make a smooth paste. Gradually add milk and chicken broth, cooking and stirring until sauce is thin and smooth.
3. Add carrots, cheese, salt, paprika, and pepper. Cover soup

and simmer for 15 minutes or until cheese is melted and carrots are slightly tender. Stir occasionally.

4. Cool at room temperature. Then refrigerate overnight in covered container.

JUST BEFORE SERVING:

1. Over low flame, heat soup carefully. Do not let it boil, lest it curdle!
2. Sprinkle parsley on soup as garnish. Top each serving with paprika. Serve immediately.

SERVES 6.

CONNOISSEUR'S MUSHROOM SOUP

The secret of this mushroom soup is the dried mushrooms. They produce a rich, strong broth that makes anything made from fresh mushrooms seem pallid by comparison. If you want an even stronger mushroom taste than the recipe yields, add some European powdered mushrooms (from the spice shelf). Also, you can add some very thinly sliced fresh mushrooms to the soup about half an hour before the simmering is done, or cook them separately and add them just before serving.

½-oz. package dried mushrooms   *4 dashes Maggi liquid seasoning*
   (imported are best)   *(optional)*
¼ cup barley   *Salt*
1 cup sour cream   *Pepper*

NIGHT BEFORE:

1. Place mushrooms into 2 qts. fast-boiling water. Reduce heat immediately. Simmer slowly, covered, for *minimum* of 2 hours. (Additional time makes broth stronger.)
2. In a separate saucepan, put barley into 2 cups boiling water. Reduce heat and simmer for 1 hour. Then drain in sieve and put barley aside.
3. Store mushroom broth and barley in separate covered containers overnight in refrigerator.

NOTE: You may want to remove mushrooms and julienne them into ⅛″ strips.

JUST BEFORE SERVING:

1. Heat mushroom broth with mushrooms. Do not boil.
2. Add barley and season with salt, pepper, and Maggi.
3. Just before serving, add sour cream and stir vigorously until lumps are dissolved.

SERVES 6.

CUCUMBER CREAM SOUP

This soup may be served hot or cold.

2 *medium cucumbers*	¼ *cup sherry*
¼ *cup chicken broth*	1 *tbsp. chopped dill*
4 *tbsp. butter*	¼ *tsp. Maggi liquid seasoning*
3 *tbsp. flour*	*(optional)*
2 *pts. half and half (or 1 pt.*	⅛ *tsp. white pepper*
milk and 1 pt. heavy cream)	¼ *tsp. salt*

NIGHT BEFORE:

1. Wash cucumbers (without peeling) and cut into large (1″) slices.
2. Put slices in blender with chicken broth and blend at high speed for 60 seconds. Now transfer them to large frying pan, add 2 tbsp. butter, and simmer for 10 minutes, stirring occasionally.
3. In a deep saucepan, melt the other 2 tbsp. butter over medium heat. Stir in flour, a little at a time, until you have a smooth paste. Then stir in all remaining liquid ingredients, followed by seasonings. Cook and continue stirring occasionally until soup thickens.
4. Add sautéed cucumbers and simmer (do not allow to boil).
5. Refrigerate overnight in covered container.

JUST BEFORE SERVING:

Hot: Bring to a simmer over medium heat, stir and serve.
Cold: Stir and serve.

SERVES 6.

EGG FLOWER SOUP

2 qts. chicken broth
1 cup celery, sliced
2 tbsp. onion, chopped
2 eggs, beaten
2 cups watercress

4 dashes Maggi liquid seasoning
   (optional)
1 tsp. salt
¼ tsp. pepper

NIGHT BEFORE:

1. In saucepan bring broth to a boil.
2. Add celery and onion and cook until boiling. At boiling point, stir in eggs, which will form a flowery pattern.
3. Add watercress and Maggi and stir at high heat for 1 minute.
4. Refrigerate in covered container overnight.

JUST BEFORE SERVING:

Heat and add salt and pepper [to taste]. Serve immediately.

S E R V E S   6 .

HOT PLUM-RUM SOUP

1 large can (1 lb., 14 ozs.)
   purple plums in heavy syrup
¼ cup brown sugar, firmly packed
1 tbsp. cornstarch
½ tsp. lemon juice
¼ tsp. salt

1 tbsp. butter
1 tbsp. rum
Several drops red food coloring
   (optional)
⅓ cup heavy cream, whipped
Nutmeg

NIGHT BEFORE:

1. Drain and measure syrup from plums. Save 1 cup. Remove pits from plums.
2. Place fruit in blender and blend until smooth.
3. In a saucepan, mix brown sugar and cornstarch. Add to this the 1 cup plum syrup, lemon juice, and salt. Cook over medium heat, stirring, until mixture is smooth and slightly thickened.
4. Stir in puréed plums. Heat through. Add butter and rum, stirring to melt butter. (Add food coloring if desired.)
5. Refrigerate overnight in covered container.

JUST BEFORE SERVING:

1. Heat gently, stirring if necessary.
2. Serve in small soup bowls or sherbet glasses, topped with whipped cream, sprinkled with nutmeg.

S E R V E S 6 .

OFF-BEAT BORSCHT

2 *cans chicken broth*	1 *tsp. black pepper*
2 *cans whole cooked beets*	2 *tbsp. Maggi liquid seasoning*
2 *tbsp. fresh dill, finely chopped*	*(optional)*
(dill weed may be substituted)	½ *tsp. powdered mushroom*
Juice of 2 lemons	2 *tbsp. granulated sugar*
2 *tsp. seasoned salt*	1 *pint sour cream*

NIGHT BEFORE:

1. In blender, combine broth and beets for 10 seconds at high speed. (You will have to blend in 2 batches because of amount of liquid.)
2. Stop blender. Stir in chopped dill. Stir in lemon juice, salt, pepper, Maggi, powdered mushroom, and sugar.
3. Simmer ingredients, in saucepan, for 15 minutes.
4. Refrigerate overnight in covered container or covered saucepan.

JUST BEFORE SERVING:

1. Heat soup. Do not boil.
2. To serve, top each portion with generous spoonful of cold sour cream, sprinkled with a little dill.

NOTE: To this soup you can add any leftover meat you have in the house. Shred meat and stir into liquid while cooking.

S E R V E S 6 .

PELMENY SIBERIAN

While this dish belongs with the soups, it is equally valid as a main course for a hearty luncheon. The pelmeny are marvelous little balls of chopped meat enclosed in delicate noodles. If you serve this as a soup, you use more broth and less pelmeny. If you serve it as a main course, you fill a plate with pelmeny, then add enough broth to fill the gaps, and top with a generous spoon of sour cream sprinkled with fresh dill. Either way it's a treat.

2 lbs. ground round of beef	2 tbsp. dill weed (or fresh
¼ lb. lard or beef fat	chopped dill)
½ cup finely chopped onion	2 cups sifted all-purpose flour
½ cup European dried mush-	1 tsp. salt
rooms, soaked in hot water 2	4 egg yolks
hours, then minced fine	1 qt. chicken broth
1 tsp. salt	Sour cream (optional)
½ tsp. fresh ground black pepper	

NIGHT BEFORE:

1. Run ground meat and fat through grinder together to blend well.
2. Knead meat with onion, mushrooms, ¼ cup water, salt, pepper, and dill weed, blending thoroughly.
3. Knead flour, salt, ½ cup water, and egg yolks together to form a paste.
4. Let paste stand for 1 hour.
5. Roll paste out very thin on lightly floured board.
6. Cut dough into 3″ squares with circular cutter.
7. Place 1 tbsp. meat mixture in center of each square.
8. Bring up sides of each square around meat and pinch together, moistening dough with a little water at edges if necessary.
9. You can now refrigerate pelmeny overnight in covered bowl and cook them just before serving. Or, you can cook them now: Drop pelmeny into large pot of boiling water (at least 4 qts.). Don't try to do them all at once—leave enough room for them to rise individually. They are done when they rise to the top (about 15 minutes). Remove with slotted spoon. Now refrigerate cooked pelmeny overnight in covered container.

JUST BEFORE SERVING:

1. Cook pelmeny if you did not do it last night.
2. Bring chicken broth to boil in large pot.

3. Reduce heat to simmer, add cooked pelmeny.
4. Serve in large soup tureen. Or, add 1 heaping tbsp. sour cream, sprinkled with more dill weed, to each plate of pelmeny.

SERVES 6.

POTAGE ST. GERMAIN
Purée of Fresh Peas Soup

3 lbs. shelled fresh peas   2 tsp. Maggi liquid seasoning
3 cups (1½ pts.) chicken broth   (optional)
1 tsp. salt   2 tbsp. butter
¼ tsp. freshly ground pepper

NIGHT BEFORE:

1. In large pot, cook peas for 5 minutes in boiling salted water.
2. Drain peas. Return to pot and mash.
3. Add broth and put in blender for 30–40 seconds at high speed or until quite smooth. (You will need to blend in 2 batches because of amount of liquid.)
4. Return to pot and put on low fire. Season with salt, pepper, and Maggi.
5. Refrigerate, covered, overnight.

JUST BEFORE SERVING:

1. Heat over low flame. Do not boil.
2. Add butter just before serving and garnish with sprinkles of cooked fresh peas, if desired.

SERVES 6.

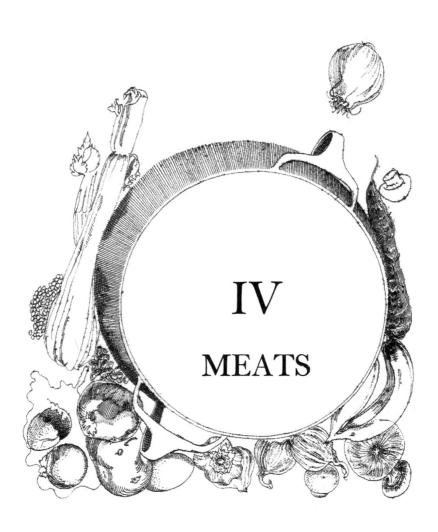

IV

MEATS

IV

BEEF 'N ALE CASSEROLE

3 lbs. stewing beef (chuck, rump, or round) cut into 2" slices
3 tbsp. olive oil
6 tbsp. butter
1 cup mushrooms, thinly sliced (about ¼ lb.)
6 medium onions, thinly sliced

3 tbsp. flour
1½ bottles dark ale
2 tsp. salt
1 tsp. black pepper
4 dashes Maggi liquid seasoning (optional)

NIGHT BEFORE:

1. Heat olive oil in heavy enameled skillet.
2. Brown meat on all sides, adding salt and pepper.
3. Remove meat to heavy casserole.
4. Add butter to skillet (do *not* remove oil). Add mushrooms, onions, and sprinkle with flour.
5. Sauté, stirring occasionally, until onions and mushrooms turn a light golden brown.
6. Put entire contents of skillet into casserole with the meat.
7. Pour in ale. Simmer over low heat for 2 hours (or until beef is tender), stirring occasionally.
8. Add salt, pepper, and Maggi.
9. Refrigerate overnight in the casserole, tightly covered. To assure retention of flavor, place plastic wrap over open casserole before putting cover on.

JUST BEFORE SERVING:

1. Remove plastic wrap and heat, covered, over medium flame until stew simmers slightly.

2. Serve with rice or mashed potatoes.

NOTE: This dish can be prepared up to 5 days before use. The flavor tends to improve with time.

SERVES 6.

BEEF STROGANOFF

1-oz. *package European dried mushrooms*

2 *lbs. very best filet of beef, trimmed of fat*

¼ *lb. butter*

¼ *cup cognac*

6 *large fresh mushrooms, sliced thin*

2 *cloves garlic minced very fine*

½ *tsp. powdered mushroom (optional)*

¼ *cup beef stock*

1 *tbsp. tomato paste*

¼ *tsp. Maggi liquid seasoning (optional)*

3 *tbsp. flour*

1½ *cups sour cream*

¼ *cup fresh chopped dill*

NIGHT BEFORE:

1. Pour 1 cup boiling water over dried mushrooms and let soak for 1 hour. Remove mushrooms, reserving stock, and chop very fine.
2. Cut filet into thin strips ¼″ by 2″ by 1″.
3. Melt half the butter in heavy skillet over medium heat. When all melted and sizzling, brown the strips of filet in butter on both sides (about a minute each side), handling the meat with tongs or a spatula, but not piercing it with a fork. It is best to do only a few pieces at a time. Remove meat to covered container and refrigerate overnight. Reserve cooking butter.
4. Add cognac to butter in which meat was cooked, and simmer 2 minutes over low flame. Add remaining butter, melt it, then add fresh mushrooms and let cook very gently for 3 minutes. Add garlic. Add chopped dried mushrooms, simmer another 2 minutes.
5. Turn off flame and add beef stock, half the reserved mushroom stock (save rest), the dried mushroom powder, tomato paste, Maggi, and flour.
6. Turn flame back on (medium) and stir slowly until sauce thickens without boiling.
7. Now beat in sour cream, a little at a time, being very careful not to allow sauce to boil. Finally, add dill.
8. Remove sauce to covered container and refrigerate overnight.

JUST BEFORE SERVING:

1. Best way to warm this dish is with a chafing dish, but top of a double boiler over simmering water will do. Heat sauce over water until steaming hot but not boiling. Stir well to make smooth. If too liquid, stir in a little more flour; if too thick, add some remaining mushroom stock.
2. When sauce is hot, put in meat, and let meat heat in sauce without increasing flame.
3. Serve direct from chafing dish, or, for formal service transfer to warm platter just before passing.

SERVES 6.

BLEU CHEESE BURGERS

3 *lbs. best ground round*
1 *egg*
1 *tsp. salt*
½ *tsp. fresh ground black*
   pepper

1 *tsp. Maggi liquid seasoning*
   (optional)
½ *cup finely chopped onion*
6 *ozs. Bleu Cheese (2 standard*
   3-oz. wedges)

NIGHT BEFORE:

1. Knead together beef, egg, salt, pepper, Maggi, and onion until well blended.
2. Divide meat into 6 equal portions. Then make 2 flat round patties, about ½" thick, out of each portion.
3. Divide cheese into 6 equal portions. Make a flat, round cake the diameter of a silver dollar out of each portion. Now place little cheese patty on each of meat patties. Then cover each with another meat patty. Pinch edges a little to seal in cheese.
4. To store overnight: Stack the 6 patties with sheets of waxed paper in between. Wrap the whole stack tightly in foil. Place in coldest part of refrigerator, or, if you plan to use them any later than next day, in freezing compartment.

JUST BEFORE SERVING:

1. If meat is frozen, thaw at room temperature. If not, just remove from refrigerator.
2. Broil, 3" from flame or filament, 4 minutes each side, and serve. (Cook longer for medium or well done.)

BOILED BEEF WITH HORSERADISH CURRANT SAUCE

3 lbs. fresh beef brisket or   ¼ cup dried currants
  2 lbs. boneless shoulder beef   2 tbsp. brown sugar
2 tsp. salt   2 tbsp. vinegar
8 peppercorns   ½ tsp. freshly grated horse-
4 raw carrots, peeled   radish
2 medium onions, peeled and   ¼ tsp. salt
  cut in half   ¼ tsp. prepared mustard
2 stalks celery, cut in pieces

NIGHT BEFORE:

1. In large pot, place beef, salt, peppercorns, carrots, onions, and celery. Pour in enough water to cover meat.
2. Cover pot. Bring water to a boil.
3. Reduce heat and simmer until meat is very tender (2–3 hours).
4. Remove meat from liquid and wrap in foil. Refrigerate overnight.
5. Strain broth, saving vegetables. Cover and store both, separately, in refrigerator overnight.

JUST BEFORE SERVING:

1. Return meat to liquid and simmer for 30 minutes.
2. Remove meat from broth. Slice thinly and keep warm.
3. Remove peppercorns from vegetables. Press vegetables through a fine strainer or purée in a blender.
4. Measure 1 cup of the beef broth into a saucepan.
5. Add vegetable purée, currants, brown sugar, vinegar, horseradish, salt, and mustard.
6. Cook over medium heat for 5 minutes, stirring to keep sauce smooth.
7. Serve beef slices immediately with hot sauce.

S E R V E S   6 .

CHILI CON CARNE

3 lbs. round or chuck steak
3 tbsp. flour
1 tsp. MSG (Monosodium Glutamate)
2 tsp. salt
½ tsp. pepper
4 tbsp. butter
3 cloves garlic

3 cups chopped onions
2 cups canned stewed tomatoes
4 slices bacon, cut into 1" pieces
5 tbsp. chili powder
2 cups canned chili beans
3 tbsp. grated Parmesan cheese
¼ cup chopped parsley

NIGHT BEFORE:

1. Cut steak into 1" cubes.
2. Toss meat cubes in mixing bowl with flour, MSG, salt, and pepper.
3. In heavy enameled saucepan, melt butter. Add meat and garlic. Brown meat lightly on all sides.
4. Add onions and sauté gently until they are transparent.
5. Add tomatoes and bacon pieces, then barely cover meat with water.
6. Mix chili powder into a paste with a little water separately, then add to saucepan. Simmer over low flame uncovered for about 3 hours, adding a little water occasionally as necessary to keep moist.
7. Remove pan from heat and let stand, covered, overnight (*not* in refrigerator).

JUST BEFORE SERVING:

1. Return pot to flame and bring to simmer. Allow to simmer about ½ hour, stirring in beans just a few minutes before serving.
2. Garnish with grated Parmesan on top, sprinkle with chopped parsley.

S E R V E S   6 .

IRISH POTATO PIE

2 *lbs. potatoes*
8 *tbsp. butter (¼ lb.)*
1 *tbsp. finely minced onions*
1½ *tsp. salt*
¼ *tsp. pepper*
2 *lbs. round steak cut into 1"*
   strips

Maggi liquid seasoning
   (optional)
1¼ *cups beef stock or rich*
   consommé
Grated Cheddar cheese
   (optional)

NIGHT BEFORE:

1. Peel potatoes, place in salted cold water, bring to boil, and boil until tender (a fork should go in easily with very little pressure).
2. Remove from water, add 5 tbsp. butter, the minced onions, salt, and pepper, and mash or blend.
3. Line a buttered baking dish (the round, about 3"-deep kind) with mashed potatoes, reserving some for top.
4. In a skillet, sauté slices of steak for about 2 minutes on each side in remaining butter.
5. Remove from skillet and place meat in center of lined dish. (Reserve butter in which meat was cooked.) Sprinkle few dashes of Maggi over meat. Then cover it with remaining mashed potatoes, like a pie crust.
6. Refrigerate pie overnight.
7. Simmer beef stock in the butter in which the meat was cooked. Refrigerate this sauce overnight in a covered container.

JUST BEFORE SERVING:

1. Remove pie from refrigerator and allow to return to room temperature.
2. Preheat oven to 350°. If desired, dot top with butter and sprinkle with grated Cheddar cheese.
3. Bake pie for 30 minutes at 350°.
4. While pie is baking, heat sauce until just simmering.
5. Remove pie from oven when done, make hole in top, and pour in sauce.

6. Serve immediately. Or, to serve buffet, keep dish hot over blazer pan of a chafing dish.

S E R V E S   6 .

MARINADE DE BOEUF NAOMI

This dish requires no cooking except to prepare the marinade. It is necessary to marinate the meat for at least 24 hours if you like it rare. For medium beef, give it 2 days to marinate, and for "done," at least 3 days.

2 *lbs. lean filet or top round of beef (have butcher trim fat and slice meat into paper-thin strips, about same thickness as veal scaloppine)*
1 *cup finely chopped onions*
2 *cloves garlic, minced*
¼ *cup olive oil*
½ *cup red wine vinegar*
½ *lb. mushrooms, finely chopped (optional)*

½ *cup dry red wine*
1 *cup beef bouillon or stock*
1 *tsp. Bovril or Maggi liquid seasoning*
1 *bay leaf*
1 *tsp. oregano*
1 *pinch of marjoram*
¼ *tsp. salt*
¼ *tsp. black pepper*
1 *cup finely chopped parsley*

NIGHT (OR TWO OR THREE NIGHTS) BEFORE:

1. Sauté onions and garlic in olive oil until golden. Then add wine vinegar and let boil down until reduced by half.

2. Stir in chopped mushrooms if desired.

3. Stir in wine, beef bouillon, and Bovril or Maggi. Add bay leaf, oregano, marjoram, salt, and pepper and simmer 5 minutes over medium heat.

4. In deep covered dish, arrange meat slices in neat layers, with a layer of the chopped parsley in between layers of meat. It is best to use the largest possible dish and have as few layers as possible. Estimate from the size of your dish how much of the parsley you can use on each layer of meat.

5. When arrangement is completed, pour boiling hot marinade over meat. Refrigerate, covered, for a minimum of 24 hours.

JUST BEFORE SERVING:

1. Remove dish of meat from refrigerator at least 1 hour before serving. It must be brought to room temperature.
2. Arrange slices of meat on platter and pour over only a little of the marinade, discarding rest.
3. Garnish with sprigs of parsley and serve.

NOTE: Any left-over slices of filet can be used to make a perfect impromptu Stroganoff. Just simmer them a few minutes in a pan with butter and a little flour, and add some sour cream at the last moment. Mushrooms are acceptable here, too.

SERVES 6.

MARINATED FILETS OF BEEF

6 12-oz. *filets of beef*	½ *tsp. allspice*
3 *slices bacon, cut in quarters*	1½ *cups olive oil*
½ *tsp. salt*	1½ *cups red wine*
¼ *tsp. black pepper*	1½ *cups cognac or Armagnac*
1 *tsp. cracked black pepper-*	¾ *cup butter*
corns	3 *tbsp. flour*
2 *bay leaves*	3 *cups beef stock*
6 *cloves*	2 *cups whole small mushrooms*

NIGHT BEFORE:

1. Make a 3″ slit in each filet, not cutting through to other side. Stuff each slit with 2 pieces of bacon, salt, and pepper.
2. Marinate filets overnight in the following mixture: peppercorns, bay leaves, cloves, allspice, olive oil, wine, cognac. This should be done in pan or dish just big enough to hold meat and liquid. Refrigerate overnight, uncovered.

JUST BEFORE SERVING:

1. Remove filets from marinade and drain on paper towels, reserving marinade.
2. Prepare sauce as follows: Melt butter in saucepan over medium heat, stir in flour, and brown (to form brown roux). Stir in beef stock and 1½ cups of reserved marinade. Add mushrooms and keep sauce hot (not boiling) while meat is cooking.

3. Broil filets under broiler to desired doneness. Or, sauté them in a little olive oil and butter in a very hot skillet, about 6 minutes each side (medium rare).
4. Arrange filets on warm platter, pour sauce with mushrooms over, and serve.

SERVES 6.

ORIENTAL BEEF WITH OYSTER SAUCE

2½ lbs. tenderloin of beef
6 tbsp. peanut or salad oil
½ cup onion, finely chopped
1 cup mushrooms, sliced
3 tsp. powdered mushroom
3 tsp. MSG

1 cup oyster sauce (several oriental and domestic brands are
available)
⅓ cup beef consommé or
1 tbsp. meat glaze
⅓ cup cornstarch

NIGHT BEFORE:

1. Slice meat into 2"-wide strips, then cut crosswise in very thin slices not over ⅛" thick.
2. In very hot skillet, sauté meat in oil for a few seconds.
3. Add onion, mushrooms, seasonings, oyster sauce, and consommé. Stir vigorously.
4. Cover and steam for 5 minutes.
5. Thicken slightly with cornstarch mixed in 3 tbsp. cold water. Cook a few seconds more, stirring constantly.
6. Refrigerate, covered, overnight.

JUST BEFORE SERVING:

1. Heat over low flame until barely simmering.
2. Serve immediately over steamed rice.

SERVES 6.

SAUERBRATEN

This is not a "night before" recipe: You must start this a *week* before.

1 4-lb. chuck roast of beef	1 tsp. whole peppercorns
2 onions stuck with cloves	½ tsp. salt
3 carrots, sliced	3 tbsp. soy sauce
1 cup brown sugar	12-oz. bottle or can dark ale
1 bay leaf	2 tbsp. flour

WEEK BEFORE:

1. Wash meat under cold water, then blot with towel. Place in heavy, deep, enameled pot (this pot must have a cover). Add onions and carrots and sprinkle brown sugar over. Add bay leaf, peppercorns, and salt, then pour in soy sauce and ale.

2. Cover tightly and allow to marinate 1 week, opening pot only once a day to turn meat completely over (use tongs or two wooden spoons). Keep in refrigerator.

NIGHT BEFORE:

Simmer for 2 hours over low heat. Then cool and refrigerate overnight.

JUST BEFORE SERVING:

1. Simmer another 30–40 minutes. Remove meat and arrange on platter with vegetables.

2. Stir flour into remaining simmering sauce and mix well to get out lumps.

3. Serve gravy separately or pour over meat on platter before serving.

S E R V E S   6 .

SIKBAJ
Baghdad Meat-Fruit Casserole

2 *tbsp. olive oil*
3 *lbs. chuck or rump, cut into*
  2" cubes
3 *cups beef consommé*
2 *tsp. cinnamon*
2 *cups carrots, sliced*
3 *cups onions, chopped*
3 *tsp. salt*

2 *tsp. freshly ground black*
  pepper
¼ *cup wine vinegar*
½ *cup honey*
1 *17-oz. can figs, drained*
1 *cup raisins*
2 *cups sliced almonds*
1 *cup parsley, chopped*

NIGHT BEFORE:

1. Heat oil in large casserole. Over low flame, lightly brown meat.
2. Add consommé, cinnamon, carrots, onions, and cook over low heat for 1½ hours. Stir occasionally.
3. Add salt, pepper, wine vinegar, and honey. Cook 1 hour. Stir occasionally.
4. Stir in figs, raisins, and almonds. Mix well and remove from heat.
5. Cover and refrigerate overnight.

JUST BEFORE SERVING:

1. Cook, covered, for 5 minutes or just enough to heat through.
2. Top with parsley and serve with rice.

SERVES 6.

SWEET AND SOUR POT ROAST

6 *medium onions, chopped*
2 *tbsp. fat*
4½ *lbs. beef rump*
Salt
Pepper
2 *bay leaves*

3 *cups beef consommé*
2 *1-lb. cans peeled whole stewed*
  tomatoes, drained
½ *cup granulated sugar*
Juice of 3 lemons

NIGHT BEFORE:

1. Fry onions in fat in large skillet until golden brown. Refrigerate in covered container overnight.
2. Season meat with salt and pepper. Brown meat in same skillet, turning on all sides.
3. Transfer to heavy enameled casserole. Add bay leaves and consommé.
4. Cover casserole and let simmer for 3–3½ hours (until nearly tender).
5. Refrigerate overnight.

JUST BEFORE SERVING:

1. Preheat oven to 350°. Add onions, tomatoes, sugar, and lemon juice to casserole.
2. Bake uncovered 20 minutes. Serve immediately, on platter, slicing meat, then spooning sauce over.

S E R V E S   6 .

TOURNEDOS WITH FOI GRAS

6 ¼" *slices foie gras*
4 *tbsp. Madeira wine*
3 *tbsp. beef stock or bouillon*
1½ *ozs. dried mushrooms,*
   soaked in boiling water
24 *slices of canned black truffle*
   (1 large truffle)
Pepper
10 *tbsp. butter, softened*

6 *filets of beef, 1" thick, tied*
   with fat
1 *tbsp. oil*
Salt
6 *thin slices white bread with*
   crusts trimmed
1 *tsp. arrowroot blended with*
   2 *tsp. Madeira*

NIGHT BEFORE:

1. Put foie gras slices in shallow plate. Cover with 2 tbsp. Madeira.
2. Add stock. Refrigerate overnight in covered dish.
3. Chop soaked mushrooms very fine, and store covered in refrigerator overnight.
4. Put truffle, 2 tbsp. Madeira, pinch of pepper, 1 tbsp. butter into small saucepan. Refrigerate, covered, overnight.

JUST BEFORE SERVING:

1. Place dish of foie gras in 150° (warming temperature) oven for 10 minutes.
2. Warm truffles over low heat.
3. Wipe filets with paper towels.
4. Melt 2 tbsp. butter and the oil in skillet over moderately high heat. Sauté filets 4 minutes on each side.
5. Remove from heat and discard strings and fat. Season with salt and pepper.
6. Toast slices of bread. Butter toasts.
7. In long shallow pan place tournedos on toasts, putting slice of foie gras (reserve stock) and several truffles on each tournedos. Keep warm.
8. To skillet, add stock and juices from foie gras and truffles.
9. Reduce liquid over medium heat to half its volume. Add arrowroot-wine mixture and simmer 1 minute.
10. Take skillet from heat and stir in 4 tbsp. butter and chopped mushrooms.
11. Pour sauce over tournedos and serve immediately.

S E R V E S 6 .

BREADED PORK CHOPS IN ORANGE SAUCE

6 trimmed pork chops　　　*¼ cup brown sugar*
4 tbsp. flour　　　*2 tbsp. grated orange rind*
6 tbsp. dry bread crumbs　　　*1 tbsp. grated lemon rind*
6 tbsp. butter　　　*1 tsp. salt*
1½ cups orange juice　　　*½ tsp. pepper*
½ cup white wine

NIGHT BEFORE:

1. Place chops in boiling salt water (at least 3 qts.). Simmer 15 minutes. Remove chops from water and drain.
2. Dust chops with a little flour, then roll in bread crumbs. Brown in heavy skillet in half the butter on both sides, then reduce heat and simmer 15 minutes.

3. In separate pan, melt rest of butter, vigorously stir in remaining flour until you have a smooth paste. Stir in orange juice and wine, and keep stirring over medium heat until smooth and thick. Add the sugar, orange rind, lemon rind, salt, and pepper. Pour sauce over chops in skillet, and simmer covered for 1 hour. Remove from heat and refrigerate overnight in same skillet, covered with foil.

JUST BEFORE SERVING:

1. Return skillet to medium heat and bring to a simmer. If sauce is too thick, stir in a little water, or more orange juice.
2. Simmer 15 minutes to heat through. Serve immediately.

S E R V E S   6 .

CHINESE ROAST PORK

This dish may be served hot or cold.

3 *lbs. boneless pork tenderloin*	4 *tbsp. soy sauce*
3 *tbsp. sherry*	3 *tbsp. brown sugar*
2 *tsp. salt*	½ *tsp. nutmeg*
1 *tsp.* MSG	1 *clove garlic, crushed*

NIGHT BEFORE:

1. Cut the pork tenderloin into 2 long strips.
2. Mix all remaining ingredients in a bowl until thoroughly blended together.
3. Pour over the pork strips in shallow dish. Marinate 4 hours in refrigerator, turning once every hour to soak in all sides evenly.
4. Drain pork.
5. Turn on broiler to high and preheat 10 minutes.
6. Broil pork strips about 4″ from flame for 1 hour, turning frequently to cook through evenly. Refrigerate cooked pork overnight.

JUST BEFORE SERVING:

Cold: Simply slice into small, ¼″-thick slices and serve.

Hot: Return to a preheated broiler for about 10 minutes, turning to heat on all sides, then slice and serve. Hot or cold, may be served with very hot mustard, chutney, other condiments.

SERVES 6.

CREAMED HAM

12 *slices cooked ham (about*   1½ *tsp. flour*
   ⅜″ *thick)*   1½ *cups chicken broth*
3 *tbsp. sweet butter*   ¾ *cup heavy cream*
1½ *cups dry white wine*

NIGHT BEFORE:

1. In a heavy skillet over low heat sauté slices of ham in butter. Do not allow ham to brown, but turn slices over at least once. Cook 15 minutes.
2. Add white wine and simmer until reduced to ¼ original volume. Then remove ham from skillet and refrigerate in covered dish overnight.
3. Stir flour quickly into pan juices until smooth and well blended, then add chicken broth and simmer very gently 10 minutes. Remove from heat and refrigerate, covered.

JUST BEFORE SERVING:

1. Bring sauce to a simmer, add heavy cream, stir, and bring to a simmer again. Do not allow to boil.
2. Add ham slices to sauce and leave about 10 minutes over low heat until meat is heated through. Serve with rice.

SERVES 6.

HAM IN ASPIC

3 *lbs. diced cooked ham*   4 *egg whites, slightly beaten*
3 *cloves garlic*   1 *tomato, cut up*
1 *tsp. thyme*   3 *tbsp. gelatin (3 envelopes)*
1 *tsp. rosemary*   1 *tbsp. chopped fresh parsley*
1 *bay leaf*   1 *tbsp. chopped pimientos*
1 *onion stuck with 4 cloves*   *Parsley for garnish*
1 *tsp. whole peppercorns*

NIGHT BEFORE:

1. Boil ham, garlic, thyme, rosemary, bay leaf, onion, and pepper-corns in 2 qts. water about 1 hour.
2. Remove ham and set aside. Strain stock and discard spices and vegetables.
3. Add slightly beaten egg whites and cut up tomato to stock, simmer 5 minutes, then strain through cheesecloth. Now dissolve gelatin in ½ cup cold water, then stir into clarified stock and quickly bring to boil. Remove from heat and set aside.
4. Arrange chopped pimientos and parsley in bottom of 2-qt. ring mold in decorative way (remember, this will be the top when you unmold it). Then pour in some of the stock to a depth of ¼″. Refrigerate mold until gelatin sets.
5. Bring out mold and arrange the ham evenly all around. Now pour in rest of stock (to cover the meat), and refrigerate mold overnight.

JUST BEFORE SERVING:

1. Dip mold briefly in hot water for no more than 10–15 seconds.
2. Place serving platter upside down over mold, then reverse quickly. If aspic doesn't slip out immediately, tap bottom of mold with wooden spoon and shake slightly.
3. Garnish platter with fresh parsley and serve with mayonnaise.

SERVES 8.

PORK SAUTÉED WITH WATERCRESS

¼ cup soybean oil	4 bunches watercress
1 lb. shoulder of pork, sliced against the grain in very thin slices	3 tbsp. soy sauce
	1 tsp. salt
	1 tsp. pepper
1 clove garlic, minced	

NIGHT BEFORE:

1. Heat oil in frying pan. Sauté pork slices and garlic lightly.
2. Refrigerate in covered dish overnight, retaining cooking oil.

JUST BEFORE SERVING:

1. Wash watercress thoroughly. Dry.
2. Reheat oil in frying pan. Finish cooking pork and garlic until golden brown.
3. Add watercress and soy sauce. Bring to a boil.
4. Cover and cook 2 minutes. Season with salt and pepper.
5. Serve immediately over steamed rice.

S E R V E S   6 .

SPARERIBS AND SAUERKRAUT CASSEROLE

6–8-lb. rack of spareribs (have   *2 medium onions, stuck with*
butcher separate ribs into seg-   *cloves*
ments of 2 ribs each)   *2 apples, cut in eighths (not*
1 tbsp. rosemary   *peeled, but cored)*
1 tbsp. whole peppercorns   *5 lbs. sauerkraut*
                                      3 pts. beer

NIGHT BEFORE:

1. Place ribs in bottom of heavy enameled casserole. Sprinkle with rosemary and peppercorns. Now arrange layer of onions and apple slices. Cover this layer with sauerkraut. Finally, pour in beer.
2. Simmer slowly covered for 3 hours without stirring. Then remove from heat and refrigerate overnight.

JUST BEFORE SERVING:

1. Place casserole over medium heat and bring to a simmer.
2. Serve immediately with boiled new potatoes.

S E R V E S   6 .

SPARERIBS WITH CREAMED HORSERADISH SAUCE

1 large rack of spareribs   *1 bay leaf*
   (6–8 lbs.)   *½ cup fresh grated horseradish*
1 tbsp. salt   *3 cups sour cream (1½ pts.)*
1 tsp. fresh ground black   *¼ cup lemon juice*
   pepper

NIGHT BEFORE:

1. With very sharp knife cut spareribs apart, either singly or in pairs.
2. Bring 6 qts. water to boil in large pot; add salt, pepper and bay leaf.
3. Drop in spareribs, bring water back to boil, then lower heat and simmer 1½ hours. Pour off water, drain ribs, and refrigerate covered overnight.

JUST BEFORE SERVING:

1. Mix horseradish, sour cream, and lemon juice in top of double boiler over simmering water. Transfer sauce to large saucepan, add ribs and heat through over moderate flame without allowing to boil.
2. Serve immediately. Goes well with parsley boiled potatoes.

SERVES 6.

SWEET-AND-SOUR PORK

1½ lbs. boneless pork loin,
 cut into 1" cubes
2 tbsp. Madeira wine
¼ cup soy sauce
3 tbsp. arrowroot
1 tbsp. flour
2 cloves garlic
6 tbsp. soybean oil
1 lb. canned pineapple chunks
 (20-oz. can)

½ cup vinegar
½ tsp. MSG
¼ tsp. pepper
2 medium carrots
4 green peppers, cut into
 1½" pieces
4 medium onions, cut in
 quarters
2 cups oil (or vegetable shortening) for deep-frying

NIGHT BEFORE:

1. Marinate pork cubes 1 hour in Madeira, 2 tbsp. soy sauce, 2 tbsp. arrowroot, and flour.
2. Crush garlic cloves and cook 2 minutes over medium heat in 1 tbsp. soybean oil. Then add juice from can of pineapple to pan. Add vinegar and rest of soy sauce, the MSG and pepper and bring to boil. Dissolve remaining 1 tbsp. arrowroot in 3 tbsp. cold water and stir into sauce. Set sauce aside off heat.

3. Peel carrots and cook in boiling salted water 10 minutes. Drain and slice into ½" slices. Sauté peppers, onions, and carrots about 5 minutes in remaining soybean oil in large skillet. Add pineapple chunks last minute of this procedure. Refrigerate cooked vegetables and pineapple overnight in covered container.

4. Deep-fry pork cubes in frying oil about 10 minutes or until golden brown. Remove from oil and drain on paper towels. Now stir meat into sauce and refrigerate overnight in covered container.

JUST BEFORE SERVING:
Combine meat in its sauce with vegetables and pineapple and heat to simmering. Serve with rice.

NOTE: This is ideal for serving in a chafing dish.
                    S E R V E S   6 .

FÅRIKÅL
Norwegian Lamb Casserole

2 *lbs. stewing lamb*	3 *tbsp. flour*
1 *large head of winter cabbage*	10 *black peppercorns*
3 *tbsp. salt*	2 *tbsp. chopped parsley*

NIGHT BEFORE:

1. Cut lamb and cabbage into 1" cubes. (If head of cabbage is very tender, simmer meat cubes in 1 cup water 45 minutes before next step.)

2. Arrange alternate layers of cabbage and lamb cubes in deep casserole, sprinkling a little salt and flour on each layer before starting next. (No harm done if you use a little more salt or flour than given in ingredients above.)

3. Add 2 cups water and the peppercorns and simmer covered over medium-low heat 1½ hours.

4. Remove from heat and refrigerate, covered, overnight.

JUST BEFORE SERVING:

1. Heat over medium heat until simmering.
2. Sprinkle with chopped parsley and serve immediately.

S E R V E S   6 .

LAMB KEBOB DELUXE
Broiled, Skewered Lamb

2½ lbs. boned leg of lamb, cut into 1" cubes
12 fresh medium mushrooms, caps removed
2 green peppers, seeded and cut into 1½" squares (save ends)
12 cherry tomatoes or 3 regular tomatoes cut in quarters (12 pineapple slices can be substituted)

1 tbsp. sesame oil
1 tbsp. olive oil
1 tsp. plus 2 tbsp. soy sauce
½ tsp MSG
6 medium onions or 12 small (1" diameter) onions
6 slices bacon, cut in thirds
2 tbsp. butter
¼ cup white wine

◆§ *MARINADE*

½ cup pineapple juice
1 tsp. soy sauce
4 tsp. lemon juice

2 cloves garlic, minced
½ tsp. freshly ground pepper

NIGHT BEFORE:

1. Combine marinade ingredients in shallow covered pan.
2. Marinate lamb cubes 2 hours, refrigerated and covered, turning frequently.
3. Remove lamb and refrigerate in separate dish, reserving marinade liquid.
4. Sauté mushroom caps, pepper squares, and tomatoes in sesame oil and olive oil over medium-low heat 5 minutes each side. Sprinkle with 1 tsp. soy sauce and MSG while cooking.
5. Refrigerate overnight in covered container.
6. Drop onions in boiling water 5 minutes. Remove and refrigerate separately.

JUST BEFORE SERVING:

1. Divide lamb cubes, bacon pieces, mushroom caps, onions, peppers, and tomatoes into 6 equal portions. Thread on individual skewers, alternating meat with vegetables. Always put piece of bacon next to onion.
2. Place skewers under broiler 4 inches from heat. Broil 6 minutes each side, basting frequently with marinade. Meat will be pink inside and extremely juicy.
3. Serve immediately on bed of rice with Sauce.

S E R V E S   6 .

TO MAKE SAUCE:

1. Place remaining marinade in saucepan. Add end pieces of green pepper, mushroom stems, any left-over pieces of onion, tomato, and bacon. Add butter, 2 tbsp. soy sauce, and wine.
2. Simmer quickly 3–4 minutes.
3. Strain and serve.

LAMB MEATBALLS IN TOMATO SAUCE

2 *lbs. boned lamb, ground very fine*	2 *cups chopped onions*
2 *tsp. salt*	½ *cup tomato paste*
½ *tsp. pepper*	¼ *cup chili sauce*
¼ *cup chopped parsley*	½ *cup diced cucumbers*
4 *tbsp. butter*	¼ *cup dry red wine*

NIGHT BEFORE:

1. In mixing bowl combine the meat, salt, pepper, and parsley and moisten with a little water. Roll into small meatballs about 1″ diameter.
2. In heavy enameled skillet, sauté meatballs in butter. Brown them on all sides.
3. Now add onions, tomato paste, chili sauce, cucumbers, and wine. Cover and simmer gently about 10 minutes. Refrigerate in covered skillet overnight.

JUST BEFORE SERVING:

1. Return skillet to flame and bring to a simmer. Heat through. Add a little water if sauce is too thick.
2. Serve immediately, with steamed white rice.

S E R V E S   6 .

LAMB WITH DILL

2 *tbsp. fat*
2 *lbs. leg of lamb, cubed*
2 *tsp. dill seed*
1 *tbsp. chopped fresh dill (dill weed can be substituted)*
1 *tsp. salt*
1 *cup beef consommé*

2 *tbsp. Maggi liquid seasoning (optional)*
3 *tbsp. flour*
1 *lb. fresh mushrooms, thinly sliced*
1 *cup sour cream*

NIGHT BEFORE:

1. Heat fat in heavy skillet. Sauté lamb cubes, turning to brown all sides.
2. Add dill seed, fresh dill, salt, consommé, and Maggi.
3. Simmer over medium heat 15–20 minutes, until lamb is tender.
4. In small bowl, mix flour and ½ cup water until smooth.
5. Stir into simmering meat. Add mushrooms.
6. Cook, covered, stirring occasionally for 15 minutes.
7. Refrigerate overnight in skillet covered with plastic wrap.

JUST BEFORE SERVING:

1. Heat until simmering. Turn off heat, stir in sour cream.
2. Serve immediately over rice.

S E R V E S   6 .

MARINATED BROILED LAMB CHOPS

6 *double lamb chops (1½" thick) or 12 small lamb chops*
1 *medium onion, sliced*
¼ *cup olive oil*
½ *cup soy sauce*
1 *garlic clove, pressed*

½ *tsp. tarragon*
1 *tsp. whole peppercorns*
1 *tsp. coarse salt*
½ *cup dry sherry*
2 *tbsp. butter*

NIGHT BEFORE:

1. Stir all ingredients except chops and butter in shallow baking dish (big enough to hold all the chops in 1 layer).
2. Add chops to marinade and refrigerate overnight, turning once during the night.

JUST BEFORE SERVING:

1. Remove chops from marinade and place on broiler pan. (Reserve marinade.) Broil chops 3" from flame or filament (or over charcoal). Broiling time depends on thickness of chops. Double chops: about 9 minutes each side for medium. Small chops: about 5 minutes each side.
2. While chops are broiling pour marinade into saucepan, bring to quick boil over high heat, add 2 tbsp. butter, and use as gravy.

SERVES 6.

MEDITERRANEAN MEAT BALLS

2 lbs. ground lamb
2 eggs, beaten
¾ cup pine nuts
¾ cup chopped parsley
2 cloves garlic, minced

¼ cup black olives, minced
¼ tsp. salt
⅛ tsp. pepper
Olive oil

NIGHT BEFORE:

1. Knead lamb, eggs, pine nuts, parsley, garlic, olives, salt, and pepper thoroughly in a bowl (preferably with bare hands). Finally add 1 tsp. olive oil and blend in.
2. Form into small meat balls (about 1" diameter), and refrigerate overnight in covered container. (Or, may be kept longer in freezer.)

JUST BEFORE SERVING:

1. Brown meat balls in olive oil, turning frequently to cook all sides. This should take about 6 minutes—you can test one by cutting open. The inside should be pink, not cooked through. Serve immediately.

2. Or, serve as an hors d'oeuvre instead of a main course. For hors d'oeuvre, put 1 tbsp. olive oil in pan of chafing dish. Allow meat balls to sizzle over low heat for about 5 minutes. Then put toothpick in each, place on buffet over very low flame to keep warm. Serve with mustard.

S E R V E S   6 .

TURKISH PILAFF

3 *lbs. boned lamb, shoulder or flank*	1 *cup pitted prunes, chopped*
3 *tbsp. butter*	1 *cup white raisins*
3 *large onions, sliced*	3 *tbsp. beef consommé (or water)*
1 *tsp. cinnamon*	2 *tbsp. melted butter*
1 *tsp. freshly ground black pepper*	4 *tbsp. lemon juice*
3 *tsp. salt*	2 *tbsp. fresh parsley, minced*
2 *cups rice*	1 *cup toasted almonds*

NIGHT BEFORE:

1. Cut lamb into small pieces. Place in heavy skillet with butter and sauté slightly. Add onions, cinnamon, and pepper. Cook over low heat, covered, for 1 hour.

2. Remove from stove, stir in 1 tsp. salt, blend, and set aside to cool.

3. In heavy saucepan, boil 4 cups water. Add rice and 2 tsps. salt. Cover, and cook 15 minutes over low heat.

4. Remove cover, place clean cloth towel over saucepan, and cook 5 minutes more over very low heat.

5. Turn off heat and cool rice 15–20 minutes.

6. During this time, cover prunes and raisins with boiling water and let stand 5 minutes. Drain.

7. When meat has cooled, spoon out as much sauce as possible and reserve in small bowl. Skim off and discard excess fat.

8. Add fruit to meat. Transfer meat to large casserole and cover with rice.

9. To meat sauce, add beef consommé and spoon over rice.

10. Bake pilaff, covered, in preheated 300° oven 40 minutes.
11. Refrigerate, tightly covered, overnight.

JUST BEFORE SERVING:
1. Blend melted butter with lemon juice.
2. Pour butter and lemon juice mixture over pilaff and toss. Top with parsley, and put casserole on top of the stove and cook over low heat until simmering.
3. Garnish with almonds and serve immediately.

S E R V E S   6 .

BORJU ES GOMBA TEKERCS
Hungarian Veal and Mushroom Rolls

1 large onion	*¼ tsp. salt*
2 tbsp. butter	*⅛ tsp. pepper*
1 lb. fresh mushrooms	*1 lb. veal scallops (6 slices)*
1 tsp. paprika	*1 cup sour cream*

NIGHT BEFORE:
1. Peel and slice onion into thin slices. Sauté slices in butter until golden.
2. Wash, drain, and slice mushrooms thinly. Add paprika to sautéed onions and stir until it dissolves. Now add sliced mushrooms. Sauté slowly over medium low heat until softened, adding salt and pepper.
3. Divide onion-mushroom mixture into 6 portions, placing 1 portion on each slice of veal. Then roll veal slices and fasten with toothpicks.
4. Place veal rolls in large skillet, add about 4 tbsp. water, and simmer over low flame, covered, about 20 minutes. Remove from heat and refrigerate, covered, overnight.

JUST BEFORE SERVING:
1. Return skillet to stove. Add sour cream to veal rolls.
2. Simmer over low flame for 30 minutes until heated through without allowing cream to boil. Serve immediately.

S E R V E S   6 .

VEAL ROLLS

6 veal cutlets (about 8" long,   3 slices white bread, crusts
    3"–4" wide)   trimmed off, torn into shreds
2 tbsp. butter   2 tbsp. olive oil
6 fresh chicken livers   ½ cup sliced fresh mushrooms
1 small onion, finely chopped   1 tbsp. flour
3" celery stalk, finely chopped   ½ cup chicken broth
¼ tsp. hickory salt   ¼ tsp. salt
                                      ⅛ tsp. pepper

NIGHT BEFORE:

1. With flat side of meat cleaver, pound each veal cutlet flat between 2 pieces of waxed paper.
2. Prepare stuffing: In butter, sauté chicken livers about 3 minutes on each side, lower heat, then add onion and celery, and simmer 3 minutes until onion softens. Then add hickory salt, bread, and 2 tbsp. water. Remove from heat, mash all ingredients together with fork, taking care to blend chicken liver well with other ingredients. Divide stuffing into 6 equal portions.
3. Now place 1 portion stuffing on end of each cutlet, roll, and tie with string at each end.
4. Heat olive oil in large skillet over high heat. Brown the 6 veal rolls quickly on all sides (2 or 3 minutes maximum). Remove veal rolls from pan with tongs, reduce heat to medium.
5. Now add mushrooms, stir in flour, add chicken broth, salt, and pepper, put back the veal rolls, cover pan, and simmer 30 minutes. Remove from heat, still covered, and refrigerate overnight.

JUST BEFORE SERVING:

1. Bring to simmer over medium heat (still covered) and cook 15 minutes.
2. Serve immediately. Steamed rice goes well with this.

SERVES 6.

VEAL STEAKS IN SOUR CREAM

1 medium onion, finely chopped
½ cup butter
6 veal steaks
Salt
Pepper

1½ cups sour cream
¼ cup chopped chives
⅔ cup shredded Provolone
(Italian Cheese)

NIGHT BEFORE:

1. In large skillet, sauté onion in 1½ tbsp. butter until golden. Remove from skillet and set aside in refrigerator overnight.
2. Season veal steaks with salt and pepper.
3. Melt remaining butter in skillet and add veal. Sauté over medium heat, turning meat until both sides are golden brown and tender.
4. Cover pan with plastic wrap and store overnight in refrigerator.

JUST BEFORE SERVING:

1. Put pan of veal on low flame and heat 10 minutes, turning meat once.
2. Remove meat from pan. Keep warm.
3. Put onion in skillet. Add sour cream, chives, and shredded cheese. Over low heat, stir mixture until cheese melts.
4. Add veal to skillet and spoon sauce over meat. Heat through and serve immediately.

SERVES 6.

ARROZ CON BANANAS
Rice and Bananas with Leftover Meat

1 lb. leftover pork or beef,
    ground and seasoned
1 clove garlic, minced
½ cup chopped onion
6 cups boiled rice

3 tsp. butter
6 bananas, cut lengthwise
Grated cheese
3 hard-boiled eggs, sliced
12 green olives, pitted

NIGHT BEFORE:

1. Mix meat with onion and garlic.
2. Place alternating layers meat and rice in well-greased casserole, finishing with layer of rice.
3. Dot liberally with butter. Cover with layer of bananas, sprinkle with grated cheese, and dot again with butter.
4. Refrigerate, covered, overnight.

JUST BEFORE SERVING:

1. Preheat oven to 375° and bake casserole 20 minutes.
2. Garnish with hard-boiled eggs and green olives. Serve immediately.

S E R V E S   6 .

HUNGARIAN GOULASH

¼ lb. bacon, diced
4 cups chopped onions
2½ lbs. lean pork loin, fat removed, cubed
1 clove garlic, minced
1 tsp. dill seed
1 tsp. paprika
½ tsp. salt

¼ tsp. pepper
3 cups sauerkraut (canned)
3 tbsp. dark brown sugar
1 lb. lean veal, cubed
2½ cups sour cream
1 tbsp. dill weed
1 tsp. Maggi liquid seasoning (optional)

NIGHT BEFORE:

1. Simmer together bacon, onions, pork, garlic, dill seed, paprika, salt, and pepper until onions are transparent.
2. Preheat oven to 350°.
3. Add sauerkraut to pot, then brown sugar, stirring just enough to blend sugar throughout.
4. Bake covered 1 hour. Stir in veal cubes and bake another ½ hour.
5. Remove from oven and refrigerate, covered, overnight.

JUST BEFORE SERVING:

1. Preheat oven to 350°.
2. Bake goulash ½ hour or until heated through.

3. Move pot to top of stove. Stir in sour cream, dill weed, and Maggi and bring back to simmer (do not allow to boil). Serve immediately.

SERVES 6.

MEAT LOAF

4 slices stale bread
½ cup milk (or half and half)
1 cup finely chopped onion
1 tbsp. butter
¼ cup chopped parsley
1 tsp. salt
½ tsp. pepper

2 tbsp. Maggi liquid seasoning
(optional)
2 eggs
1 lb. each: ground beef,
ground veal, ground pork
½ cup bread crumbs
4 slices bacon
Red wine (optional)

NIGHT BEFORE:

1. Trim crusts from bread and soak in milk.
2. Sauté chopped onion in butter until transparent but not browned.
3. Knead soaked bread, onion, parsley, salt, pepper, Maggi, and eggs into ground meat until all ingredients are well blended.
4. Shape meat into a loaf in shallow roasting pan. Sprinkle with bread crumbs, lay slices of bacon on top.
5. Preheat oven to 400°. Bake meat loaf 30 minutes. Remove from oven, cover with foil, and refrigerate overnight.

JUST BEFORE SERVING:

1. Preheat oven to 350°.
2. Remove foil and bake meat loaf uncovered 30 minutes, basting occasionally.
3. Remove loaf to hot serving platter and discard bacon strips.
4. Add a little water or red wine (or both) to pan drippings, hold pan over flame and boil for a moment, scraping bits of meat into liquid. Pour this gravy into gravy boat and serve with meat loaf.

NOTE: For delicious leftovers, try cold sliced meat loaf or meat loaf sandwiches.

SERVES 6.

SPANISH MEAT BALLS

½ lb. Spanish chorizo sausage (or   ½ tsp. salt
   other equally strong garlic   6 tbsp. dry bread crumbs
   sausage)   1 beaten egg
¾ lb. ground boned lamb   2 tbsp. olive oil
½ lb. ground beef   1 cup chopped onion
1 clove garlic, minced   ½ cup tomato paste
2 tbsp. chopped parsley   1 cup red wine

NIGHT BEFORE:

1. Run sausages through fine blade of meat grinder.
2. Knead ground sausage with ground lamb and beef. Then work in (with hands) garlic, parsley, salt, bread crumbs, and beaten egg. Form mixture into 1″ meat balls.
3. Brown meat balls on all sides quickly in olive oil. Then remove meat balls, reserving cooking oil, and store in covered container in refrigerator overnight.
4. Now place chopped onion in skillet and sauté until transparent. Stir in tomato paste, ½ cup water, and wine. Simmer about 5 minutes, remove, cover, and store overnight in refrigerator.

JUST BEFORE SERVING:

1. Add meat balls to sauce, bring slowly to simmer over medium heat, and cook about 15 minutes.
2. Remove to serving platter and serve immediately. Goes well with rice or noodles.

S E R V E S   6 .

TÖLTÖTT KÁPOSZTA
Hungarian Stuffed Cabbage

1 medium head fresh cabbage   ¼ tsp. pepper
1 medium onion, minced   ½ tsp. paprika
1 tbsp. butter   1 cup sauerkraut
½ lb. ground beef   1½ cups tomato purée
½ lb. ground pork   Spareribs or slices of bacon
1 cup rice (washed, uncooked)   (optional)
½ tsp. salt

1. Core head of cabbage. Parboil by dropping it into pan of rapidly boiling salted water and boiling for 2 or 3 minutes. Remove from water and drain.
2. Sauté minced onion in butter until golden. Remove heat.
3. In mixing bowl, blend beef, pork, sautéed onion, and rice. Add salt, pepper, and paprika.
4. Removing 1 cabbage leaf at a time, remove large central vein, then place 2 tbsp. meat mixture in each leaf and roll securely, tucking flap in. Continue until cabbage and meat are used up.
5. Place sauerkraut in bottom of heavy enameled pot, the deeper the better. Spread it out to make a layer.
6. Now set in the cabbage rolls, flap side down. Add few loose spareribs or bacon slices, if desired for additional flavor.
7. Spread tomato purée over top of cabbage rolls, then add boiling water to cover by about 1".
8. Simmer 1 hour.
9. Remove from heat and refrigerate covered overnight.

JUST BEFORE SERVING:
1. If there is not enough liquid and cabbage may burn in reheating, add a little water or beef stock.
2. Spareribs or bacon may be added at this point.
3. Bring to a simmer over medium heat and serve.

SERVES 6.

COLD TONGUE WITH HORSERADISH SAUCE

1 5-lb. fresh tongue	¼ lb. butter
1 large onion, sliced	¼ cup flour
2 sprigs parsley	½ cup sherry
1 leek	½ pt. heavy cream
1 stalk celery	4 tbsp. fresh grated horseradish
1 carrot, peeled	⅛ tsp. paprika

NIGHT BEFORE:
1. Wash tongue, trim off gristle, fat, and any bones adhering to

thick end. Place in heavy enameled saucepan, cover with salted
water, add onion, parsley, leek, celery, and carrot. Simmer
1 hour.

2. Remove tongue from liquid (reserve liquid). Remove skin
from tongue.

3. In Dutch oven, melt butter and brown the skinned tongue on
all sides in butter.

4. Now sprinkle with flour, add sherry and reserved liquid to cover
tongue. Simmer over medium heat for about 2½ hours until
tender. Remove tongue and refrigerate in covered dish overnight.

JUST BEFORE SERVING:

1. Slice tongue into slices ⅛"–¼" thick and arrange on serving
platter on bed of lettuce.

2. Whip cream until soft peaks are formed. Blend in grated horseradish and paprika. Spread sauce over cold tongue slices and
serve.

SERVES 6.

V
POULTRY

V

BRAZILIAN RICE WITH CHICKEN

6 slices bacon, uncooked
1 small (2 lbs.) frying chicken,
  cut in pieces
1 onion, chopped
1 tbsp. salt
2 tomatoes, peeled and cut in
  pieces

6 pork sausages, cut in pieces
2 cups uncooked rice
6 cups chicken broth
1 tbsp. chopped parsley
1 tbsp. chopped chives
½ tsp. pepper

NIGHT BEFORE:

1. Cut up bacon into small pieces and put into large, heavy frying pan. Add cut-up chicken.
2. Brown meat until chicken is golden. Add onion, salt, tomatoes, sausages, and rice.
3. Fry 12 minutes.
4. Refrigerate overnight in covered dish.

JUST BEFORE SERVING:

1. Add broth, parsley, chives, and pepper and cook over medium heat 15–25 minutes until broth is almost absorbed. (*Note:* The rice should be moist.)
2. Serve immediately.

SERVES 6.

BROILED CHICKEN NIGHT BEFORE

3 small broiling chickens, split
  into halves
4 tbsp. butter
2 tbsp. lemon juice

2 tbsp. soy sauce
¼ tsp. pepper
½ tsp. salt
¼ cup red wine

NIGHT BEFORE:

1. Preheat broiler.
2. Broil chicken halves about 20 minutes, beginning with skin side down and turning occasionally. While broiling, baste with mixture of all remaining ingredients, warmed enough to melt butter. Baste frequently, reserving only about ¼ basting liquid for next day.
3. When brown, refrigerate chicken in covered container overnight.

JUST BEFORE SERVING:

1. Preheat oven to 350°.
2. Arrange pieces of chicken, skin side up, in roasting pan.
3. Warm up basting mixture, and coat pieces of chicken with it, using it all up.
4. Bake 20 minutes until hot; serve immediately.

S E R V E S 6 .

CHICKEN COTELETTES POLONAISE WITH DILL SAUCE

These little chicken delights are a wonderful party dish. They are easy to serve at a sit down dinner, but also keep perfectly well on a buffet in a chafing dish. They are delicious leftovers—in fact, some people prefer them cold, cut in slices, and served on a bed of lettuce garnished with mayonnaise. They also travel well cold, and are ideal for outings and picnics.

3 *slices soft white bread*	10 *dashes Maggi liquid seasoning (optional)*
3 *cups chicken broth*	¼ *tsp. salt*
¼ *lb. melted butter*	⅛ *tsp. freshly ground pepper*
3 *lbs. ground chicken meat, boned and skinned*	¼ *cup flour*
3 *eggs*	*Shortening*
4 *tbsp. fresh dill (dill weed can be substituted)*	½ *pt. heavy cream*

NIGHT BEFORE:

1. Soak bread 2 minutes in 1 cup chicken broth and the melted butter. Save liquid.

2. Combine chicken, eggs, bread, and 2 tbsp. dill by stirring until well blended. Knead with hands if necessary. Add Maggi. Mixture should be loose in texture.

3. Refrigerate 1 hour before adding salt and pepper. This can be
   ' the stopping point until next day, or you can continue with the following steps:

4. Make spherical patties (not flat) about 1½" in diameter.

5. Roll in flour and fry with shortening in heavy pan (cast iron or enamel). Cook 4 minutes on each side, or until top and bottom are golden brown.

6. Place in covered bowl and refrigerate overnight.

JUST BEFORE SERVING:

1. If you stopped at step 3, proceed with steps 4 and 5 above, then 2 and 3 below.

2. Or, if you fried the cotelettes last night, place in ovenproof dish in 275° oven. Add enough heavy cream to half cover cotelettes, sprinkle with 2 tbsp. dill.

3. Bake 45 min. and serve with rice, using the liquid in the dish as a sauce.

S E R V E S   6 .

CHICKEN LIVERS IN TOMATO CREAM

1 lb. chicken livers	2 whole cooked tomatoes
1 large onion, peeled and thinly sliced	¼ tsp. crumbled dried sweet basil
¼ lb. butter	1½ cups heavy cream
Salt	Crisp buttered toast points made
Pepper	from 8 slices light rye bread
¼ lb. fresh mushrooms, thinly sliced	Chopped parsley

NIGHT BEFORE:

1. In frying pan over medium heat, sauté onions and chicken livers in butter for 10 minutes, until onions are tender and livers are lightly brown and barely cooked.

2. Season with salt and pepper. Add mushrooms and tomatoes (drained, if you are using canned tomatoes). Continue cooking, turning, until mushrooms are tender.
3. Sprinkle with basil. Reduce heat, and pour in cream. Cook until mixture simmers, gently stirring occasionally.
4. Continue cooking 5 minutes until liquid is slightly reduced.
5. Refrigerate in covered container overnight.

JUST BEFORE SERVING:
1. Heat up mixture over low flame until just simmering.
2. Taste; add additional salt and pepper, if necessary.
3. Spoon over crisp toast points and sprinkle each serving lightly with parsley.
4. Serve immediately.

NOTE: This is an ideal chafing dish recipe.

S E R V E S 6.

CHICKEN-NOODLE CASSEROLE

½ lb. dried egg noodles
3 cups cooked ground chicken
* (or turkey)*
¼ cup chicken stock
½ cup bread crumbs
½ cup thinly sliced fresh
* mushrooms*
1 oz. dried mushrooms (soaked
* 1 hour in boiling water, then*
* chopped very fine)*
3 eggs
⅛ tsp. thyme
¼ tsp. rosemary
½ tsp. salt
¼ tsp. pepper
½ cup grated Parmesan cheese
Chopped parsley

NIGHT BEFORE:
1. Drop noodles into 3 qts. rapidly boiling salted water and boil 7 minutes.
2. Butter a 2-qt. casserole. Arrange noodles on bottom.
3. Mix together ground chicken, bread crumbs, both kinds of mushrooms, eggs, chicken stock, thyme, rosemary, salt, pepper. Make layer of this mixture over noodles in casserole.

4. Add layer of Parmesan cheese over top, distributed evenly.
5. Cover with waxed paper and refrigerate overnight.

JUST BEFORE SERVING:

1. Preheat oven to 400°.
2. Bake 20 minutes and serve, garnished with chopped parsley.

SERVES 6.

CHICKEN-PINEAPPLE CURRY

4 *cups cooked chicken, diced*   ½ *tsp. freshly ground black*
2 *medium onions, chopped*   *pepper*
1 *stalk celery, chopped*   ½ *tsp. dry mustard*
2 *apples, peeled, cored, and*   1 *bay leaf*
  finely chopped   3 *cups chicken broth*
6 *tbsp. butter*   2 *cups pineapple chunks, fresh*
¼ *cup flour*   *or canned*
3 *tsp. curry powder*   1 *cup light cream*
1½ *tsp. salt*   3 *tsp. Maggi liquid seasoning*
                                       (optional)

NIGHT BEFORE:

1. In large skillet sauté onion, celery, and apple in butter until tender (but not browned).
2. Sprinkle on flour and curry powder and cook 3 minutes.
3. Add salt, pepper, mustard, and bay leaf. Gradually stir in chicken broth. Bring this to a boil.
4. Simmer slowly 15 minutes, stirring occasionally.
5. Remove bay leaf. Add pineapple and cream. Cook 2 minutes.
6. Store in covered container overnight in refrigerator.

JUST BEFORE SERVING:

1. Add chicken to mixture and cook until heated through.
2. Just before serving add Maggi. Stir.
3. Serve over rice with chutney.

SERVES 6.

COQ AU VIN
Chicken in Wine Sauce

2 *medium onions, sliced*
1 *clove of garlic, finely minced*
3 *carrots*
1 *leek*
2 *full bottles dry red wine*
2 *bay leaves*
8 *tbsp. butter*

2 *3-lb. fryers (have butcher cut them into breasts, legs, and wings, and make a separate package of necks, wing tips, and giblets)*
1 *tbsp. flour*

NIGHT BEFORE:

1. Peel carrots and cut into ¼" slices.
2. Wash and slice leek, cutting off and discarding green top.
3. In heavy enameled saucepan, sauté carrots, leek, onions, and garlic in 2 tbsp. butter until onion is soft and transparent but not browned.
4. Add chicken giblets, wing tips, and necks, and brown with vegetables.
5. Add wine and bay leaves and simmer over very low flame 3 hours.
6. While sauce is simmering, in a heavy skillet sauté breasts, legs, and wings of chickens in 4 tbsp. butter about 15 minutes, browning on all sides. Remove from heat and refrigerate overnight in tightly covered container.
7. When wine sauce is done, strain it, and refrigerate, covered, overnight.

JUST BEFORE SERVING:

1. Bring sauce to simmer over medium-low flame. Thicken with flour blended with remaining 2 tbsp. butter.
2. Add sautéed chicken to sauce and simmer covered 40 minutes. Serve with rice.

SERVES 6.

LEMON CHICKEN

2 *young frying chickens (about*   2 *tbsp. chopped fresh chives or*
  3 lbs. each)   *young scallions*
1 *large onion, cut up*   1 *tsp. salt*
3 *stalks celery, cut up*   1 *tsp. freshly ground pepper*
3 *carrots, cut up*   4 *dashes Maggi liquid season-*
1 *tbsp. rosemary*   *ing (optional)*
1 *bay leaf*   1 *cup parsley, chopped*
                                      2 *tbsp. butter*

NIGHT BEFORE:

1. Place *whole* chickens in bottom of 12-qt. covered stock pot. Cover with all the vegetables. Add seasonings and butter.
2. Pour in cold water to cover chickens by 1″.
3. Bring to boil, then reduce to simmer. Simmer, covered, 1½ hours.
4. Remove chicken from pot and store overnight in covered receptacle. Store cooking liquid separately.

JUST BEFORE SERVING:

1. Make lemon sauce.
2. Add cooked chicken, having separated major pieces, to hot sauce.
3. Serve over rice, garnished with chopped parsley.

SERVES 6.

⋖§ *LEMON SAUCE FOR CHICKEN*

4 *lemons*   1 *cup very strong chicken broth*
⅛ *lb. butter*   ½ *tsp. salt*
4 *tbsp. flour*   ¼ *tsp. white pepper*
2 *packages dried chicken-noodle*   2 *tbsp. powdered sugar*
  soup

1. Grate rinds of lemons and set aside. Squeeze juice and do same.
2. Melt butter in top of double boiler over simmering water. Add flour and stir to smooth paste.

3. Add the grated lemon rinds and paste (not the noodles) from soup packages. Stir continually.
4. Little by little add chicken broth, stirring all the while, until sauce acquires desired consistency. If more liquid is needed, use some of the cooking liquid from the chickens, strained.
5. Add lemon juice to taste, salt, pepper, and sugar.
6. Keep hot in double boiler.

MAKES ABOUT 2 CUPS.

PAPRIKA CHICKEN

1 cup chopped onions	½ tsp. salt
2 tbsp. butter	¾ cup chicken broth
1 tbsp. paprika	½ cup sour cream
6 lbs. chicken pieces (breasts, legs, thighs)	

NIGHT BEFORE:

1. Sauté onions in butter until barely beginning to brown.
2. Turn heat down to low, stir in paprika, mixing well.
3. Put in pieces of chicken and cook slowly for 25 minutes, turning occasionally. Now add salt and chicken broth (which should be heated almost to boiling point before adding).
4. Cover pan and simmer slowly 1 hour.
5. Remove from heat and refrigerate, covered, overnight.

JUST BEFORE SERVING:

1. Put pan over medium heat and bring to simmer.
2. Stir in sour cream.
3. Again bring barely to simmer. *Important:* Do not allow to boil after adding sour cream, because it will separate.

SERVES 6.

DUCK IN MUSHROOM SAUCE

2 5-lb. ducks, ready for roasting   1 lb. mushrooms
2 tsp. salt   ¼ cup olive oil
¼ tsp. pepper   ¼ lb. butter
1 cup chopped onions   2 tbsp. flour
1 clove garlic, minced very fine   1 cup chicken broth

NIGHT BEFORE:

1. Rub ducks with salt and pepper. Preheat oven to 375°. Roast ducks 2 hours, removing fat from bottom of pan as it drips.
2. Allow ducks to cool after roasting, then disjoint them, separating legs, thighs, breasts. Refrigerate pieces of duck overnight.
3. Prepare onions and garlic. Wash mushrooms, then slice them thinly. Refrigerate these ingredients too.

JUST BEFORE SERVING:

1. Sauté onions, garlic, and mushrooms in covered skillet in olive oil and butter, reserving 2 tbsp. butter for later. Stir occasionally to expose all mushroom slices to heat evenly.
2. When mushrooms are soft, but not burned or browned, add pieces of duck to skillet.
3. Melt reserved 2 tbsp. butter, stir in flour to make a smooth paste, then slowly add chicken broth, stirring vigorously. Now add this sauce to large skillet and cover. Simmer duck, mushrooms, and sauce about 30 minutes, uncovered. If sauce seems to thicken too much, add a little more chicken broth.
4. Serve with rice or egg noodles.

SERVES 6.

ROAST SQUAB WITH WILD RICE STUFFING

This recipe is for 1 squab. It may be multiplied for any number, allowing 1 squab per person.

½ tsp. salt	*2 tbsp. white raisins*
⅓ cup wild rice	*2 tbsp. butter*
1 fresh cleaned squab (with	*1 strip bacon, cut in half*
giblets separate)	*⅓ cup chicken broth*

NIGHT BEFORE:

1. Bring 2 cups water to boil. Add salt, then stir in wild rice. Cook over medium-low flame 40 minutes until tender. Remove from heat.
2. Pass squab livers twice through finest blade of meat grinder. This will produce almost a purée. Stir purée into wild rice off heat. Now add raisins and mix with rice. Set rice aside.
3. Butter outside and inside cavity of squab, stuff squab with wild rice, and tie. Now place 2 pieces bacon, overlapping each other lengthwise about ⅛" over each side of breast.
4. Preheat oven to 450°. Place squab on rack in roasting pan (uncovered) and put in oven. Immediately reduce heat to 350°. Roast squab 30 minutes and remove, cover pan with foil, and refrigerate overnight.

JUST BEFORE SERVING:

1. Preheat oven to 350°. Remove foil and return squab to oven. After 10 minutes pour chicken broth into roasting pan and remove bacon strips.
2. Roast another 10 minutes, basting frequently.
3. Remove squab to warm platter and with potholder hold pan with drippings over medium flame. Tip pan and scrape drippings into juices at one end. If too dry, add a little more broth. Bring to quick boil and transfer to gravy boat. Serve squab and gravy immediately. It is best to cut open squab first, exposing stuffing, and spoon gravy over meat *and* stuffing.

SERVES 1.

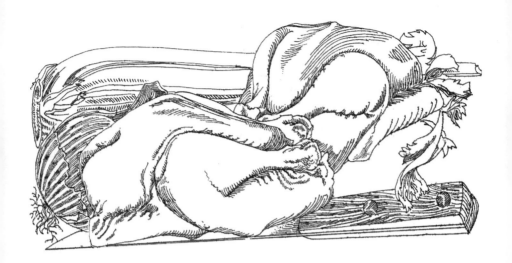

ROCK CORNISH GAME HENS À LA CRÊME

6 Rock Cornish game hens	3 tbsp. sherry
½ cup butter	2 stalks celery
½ tsp. salt	2 sprigs parsley
¼ tsp. white pepper	2 tbsp. cognac or brandy
1½ lbs. onions, peeled and sliced very thin	¾ cup heavy cream

NIGHT BEFORE:

1. Thaw out hens if frozen. Remove livers and giblets. Split hens in half.
2. In Dutch oven, brown hen halves in butter, season with salt and pepper. Remove browned pieces and set aside.
3. Put onions in Dutch oven, then add wine, celery, parsley, and cognac and finally the hen halves. Simmer slowly, covered, about 25 minutes.
4. Refrigerate, covered, overnight.

JUST BEFORE SERVING:

1. Return Dutch oven to fire and bring to simmer. Remove hen halves and keep warm separately. Remove celery and parsley and discard.
2. Stir cream slowly into onions and drippings, simmer until hot but do not boil.
3. Pour cream sauce over hen halves on warm platter and serve immediately.

SERVES 6.

VI

FISH AND SEAFOOD

VI

BROILED SHRIMPS

3 dozen medium-to-large
  shrimps
½ cup soy sauce
1 cup dry white wine

3 cloves garlic
1 tsp. seasoned salt (Lawry's)
1 cup melted butter
½ cup dry bread crumbs

NIGHT BEFORE:

1. Peel and devein shrimps, leaving last segment of shell and tail shells on ends. Now, starting at large end of each shrimp, split it halfway up to tail, cutting into groove left by vein.
2. Now arrange shrimps in shallow roasting pan. Place first shrimp at edge, with tail sticking up, leaning against side of pan, and the two split "legs" lying flat. Stand next shrimp up in "V" of first, and so on. Depending on length of pan, you should end up with 2 or 3 rows.
3. Pour soy sauce and wine over shrimps, making sure to wet them all.
4. Peel and mince garlic very fine, sprinkle bits of garlic over all shrimps.
5. Sprinkle seasoned salt evenly over all. Refrigerate pan as is overnight.

JUST BEFORE SERVING:

1. Preheat broiler.
2. Pour melted butter over all shrimps, being careful to wet upper surfaces of all of them.
3. Sprinkle dry bread crumbs over all shrimps.
4. Put under broiler 10–15 minutes. They are ready when liquid

in pan is sizzling, upper surfaces of shrimps are slightly browned, and tops of tail shells are beginning to char.

5. Remove shrimps to warm platter with spatula and serve with liquid in pan as sauce.

SERVES 6.

COLD POACHED TROUT

6 *small fresh trout, cleaned,* *with heads removed*
3 *lemons*
1 *tsp. fresh ground white* *pepper*
6 *tsp. rosemary*

Salt
1 *cup dry white wine*
1 *cup fish stock or clam juice*
1 *tbsp. butter*
½ *cup finely chopped onion*

NIGHT BEFORE:

1. Wash trout in cold water, blot dry. Slash outside flesh diagonally, 2 or 3 cuts to each fish.
2. Cut lemons in half. Using ½ lemon for each trout, gently rub with cut side of lemon, squeezing as you rub. Season inside and out with salt and pepper, then sprinkle 1 tsp. rosemary in the cavity of each fish.
3. Bring wine, stock, butter, and onion to simmer in shallow skillet. Add fish and simmer 12–15 minutes (no more). Refrigerate, in skillet, 1 hour. When cool, remove fish carefully from liquid, lift off skin, and store fish on bed of paper towels in dish, covered with foil or plastic film. Refrigerate liquid separately.

JUST BEFORE SERVING:

1. Arrange trout on beds of lettuce on individual serving plates.
2. Pour over each fish 1 tsp. of the liquid. Serve with mustard mayonnaise.

SERVES 6.

CURRIED SHRIMPS

2 lbs. fresh shrimps
6 tbsp. butter
1 medium onion, sliced thinly
1/4 tsp. salt
Dash Tabasco sauce
Pinch white pepper
1 bay leaf, crumbled

1 1/2 tbsp. curry powder (for medium-strength curry flavor; for stronger curry add up to 3 tbsp.)
1 1/2 tbsp. flour
2 cups clam juice
1 tbsp. tarragon

NIGHT BEFORE:

1. Peel and devein shrimps. Drop them into boiling water (about 3 qts.) and boil 5 minutes. Remove from water and drain.
2. Melt butter and sauté onion until transparent. Add salt, Tabasco, pepper, bay leaf, curry powder, flour. Stir thoroughly, and cook about 10 minutes. Stir in clam juice.
3. Run entire mixture from step 2 through blender 60 seconds at high speed to make purée. Return to heat and add tarragon and cooked shrimps. Refrigerate in covered container overnight.

JUST BEFORE SERVING:

1. Heat curried shrimps in top of double boiler over simmering water. Stir frequently, If sauce is a little too gummy, add some clam juice.
2. Serve with white steamed rice and chutney.

NOTE: This is an ideal chafing dish recipe, perfect for buffets. Also, lobster or crabmeat can be added or substituted.

S E R V E S   6 .

DEVILED CRABMEAT

2 *cups lump crabmeat (cooked)*   ½ *tsp. salt*
1¼ *cup bread crumbs*   ¼ *tsp. dry mustard*
½ *cup milk*   6 *drops Tabasco sauce*
1 *cup sour cream*   ¼ *cup olive oil*
1 *tbsp. Worcestershire sauce*   2 *tbsp. butter*

NIGHT BEFORE:

1. Soak 1 cup bread crumbs in milk for 10 minutes. Remove to mixing bowl.
2. Add sour cream, Worcestershire sauce, salt, mustard, Tabasco, and olive oil, and mix thoroughly.
3. Fold crabmeat into mixture gently to avoid breaking up meat too much. Butter 6 ramekins, divide crabmeat mixture evenly into them, and refrigerate overnight, covered with waxed paper.

JUST BEFORE SERVING:

1. Preheat oven to 400°.

2. Sprinkle remaining ¼ cup bread crumbs over tops of ramekins, then dot them with butter.
3. Bake 15 minutes; serve immediately.

S E R V E S   6 .

GELATINA DE CAMARÃRO E LANGOSTA
Shrimp Gelatin with Lobster Mayonnaise

2 lbs. fresh shrimps	3 tbsp. butter
2 cups lemon juice	1½ cups cooked lobster meat
2 cups white wine	4 tbsp. lobster paste (canned)
2 carrots, sliced	3 tsp. salt
1 bay leaf	2 cups mayonnaise seasoned with
1 clove garlic, minced	½ tsp. mustard powder
1 tsp. salt	Lettuce for garnish
2 envelopes unflavored gelatin	Parsley, lemon and pineapple
2 egg whites, beaten to soft	slices for garnish (optional)
peaks	

NIGHT BEFORE:

1. Shell shrimps, remove heads, clean, and let soak in lemon juice.
2. Simmer heads and shells 40 minutes in 1 cup water and the wine, adding carrots, bay leaf, garlic, and salt. Strain through damp cloth.
3. In small bowl, sprinkle gelatin on 1 cup cold water and leave until water is absorbed.
4. Put shrimp and wine broth back on stove, and on low heat, add gelatin, stirring until dissolved.
5. Remove from stove. Add beaten egg whites and let stand 30 minutes. Then strain through damp cheesecloth.
6. Meanwhile, fry shrimps in butter. Set shrimp aside to cool.
7. Pour 1″ of gelatin mixture into 2-qt. mold. Put in refrigerator to set.
8. Once set, add some shrimps and cover with another inch of gelatin. Repeat setting process.

9. Repeat layers of shrimp and gelatin in this manner until used up. Refrigerate overnight.

JUST BEFORE SERVING:
1. Mix lobster meat and paste with seasoned mayonnaise.
2. Unmold shrimp gelatin by setting mold in hot water for a few seconds. Put gelatin onto large plate, surrounded with lobster mayonnaise.
3. Garnish with lettuce leaves, parsley, lemon and pineapple slices if desired.

SERVES 6.

JAMBALAYA

2 cups shrimps, cleaned and
   cooked
2½ tbsp. butter
2 large onions, diced
1 tbsp. flour
2 cups hot clam consommé or
   clam juice
1 can (1 lb.) tomatoes, cooked
   and peeled, plus their juice
1 clove garlic, pressed
1 tbsp. parsley, chopped

1 tsp. salt
1 tsp. pepper
1 cup rice, uncooked
⅛ tsp. saffron
1 bay leaf
1 green pepper, chopped
1 red pepper, chopped
1 cup sherry (optional)
1 cup oysters, shucked
1 cup clams

NIGHT BEFORE:
1. Melt butter in heavy skillet. Add onion and sauté until browned.
2. Slowly add flour. Stir until browned.
3. Add consommé or clam juice, stirring constantly to form a smooth paste.
4. Add tomatoes with their juice, pressed garlic clove, parsley, salt, pepper, rice, saffron, bay leaf, green pepper, and red pepper.
5. In covered skillet, cook over low heat 20–30 minutes, until rice is tender and has absorbed most of liquid.
6. Add shrimps, then oysters and clams with their liquor. Cover and heat 5 minutes.

7. Refrigerate, covered, overnight.

JUST BEFORE SERVING:

1. Heat covered until edges of oysters are curled.
2. Add sherry if desired, heat 2 minutes, and serve immediately.

S E R V E S   6 .

JANSON'S FRA STELSE
Norwegian Anchovy Pie

2 *medium onions, sliced very*   18 *anchovy filets*
   thin   1 *tsp. white pepper*
3 *tbsp. butter*   ½ *pt. heavy cream*
1 *lb. potatoes*

NIGHT BEFORE:

1. Sauté onions in 2 tbsp. butter over medium-low heat until golden. Peel and grate potatoes.
2. In buttered pie dish arrange thin layer of grated potatoes, then one of onions, then anchovies, finally a top layer of potatoes. Dot with remaining butter and sprinkle white pepper over top.
3. Place in preheated 300° oven for total of 50 minutes. After first 10 minutes pour half the cream over pie; 10 minutes later pour on the rest.
4. Remove from oven and refrigerate, covered, overnight.

JUST BEFORE SERVING:

Heat in preheated 300° oven 10–15 minutes and serve immediately.

Note: This is a good luncheon or light supper dish, served with a salad and beverage.

S E R V E S   6 .

JAPANESE TEMPURA SHRIMPS

2 lbs. fresh shrimps
½ cup soy sauce
½ cup sweet sherry
2 tsp. sugar
½ tsp. salt
½ tsp. dry ginger

4 cups oil or vegetable shortening for deep-frying
2 eggs
2 cups flour
4 tbsp. (½ stick) butter

NIGHT BEFORE:
1. Peel and devein shrimps, but leave little tail shells on. Wash in cold water and drain on paper towels. Make sure shrimps are dry. Refrigerate overnight in tightly covered container.
2. Mix together ½ cup water, the soy sauce, sherry, sugar, salt, and ginger. Refrigerate overnight, covered.

JUST BEFORE SERVING:
1. Bring deep-frying fat to 375°.
2. In bowl, beat eggs with whisk, then beat in flour and 1 cup water.
3. Holding shrimps by the tail, dip in batter, then deep-fry about 5 minutes or until golden brown. While fried shrimps are draining on paper towels, heat soy sauce mixture to simmer and stir in butter.
4. Serve hot shrimps with individual cup of sauce for each person for dipping.

SERVES 6.

LINGUINE WITH WHITE CLAM SAUCE

1 cup chopped onions
1 clove garlic, minced
¼ cup olive oil
3 7½-oz. cans minced clams
1½-pt. bottle clam juice

¼ cup chopped chives
4 tbsp. butter
½ tsp. black pepper
1½ lbs. linguine (or thin spaghetti)

NIGHT BEFORE:

1. Sauté onions and garlic in olive oil until onions are transparent but not browned.
2. Add clams with their juice, reduce heat to low, and simmer, covered, about 30 minutes. Stir in chives, butter, and pepper. Refrigerate, covered, overnight.

JUST BEFORE SERVING:

1. Cook linguine or spaghetti in boiling salted water according to package directions.
2. Drain and transfer to top of double boiler over simmering water.
3. Add white clam sauce, stir gently, and cover, to heat thoroughly.
4. If sauce is not liquid enough, add some of the bottled clam juice.
5. Serve steaming hot in warm platter.

SERVES 6.

LOBSTER IN SHERRY CREAM SAUCE

3 2-lb. lobsters (boiled in shell)   3 tbsp. brandy
6 tbsp. butter   6 egg yolks
½ tsp. salt   2 cups cream
⅛ tsp. white pepper   6 tbsp. sherry
⅛ tsp. paprika

NIGHT BEFORE:

1. Remove meat from tails and claws of boiled lobsters and cut in ½" pieces.
2. In large skillet, melt butter, add lobster meat and heat (without browning) 3 or 4 minutes. Add seasonings.
3. Warm brandy away from skillet, then pour over lobster and flame, shaking pan back and forth until flame dies.
4. Beat egg yolks with cream, then add sherry and mix well. Now add this sauce to lobster in pan and stir over low heat until sauce thickens. Cover and refrigerate overnight.

JUST BEFORE SERVING:

1. Transfer lobster in sauce to top of double boiler. Heat through over simmering water, stirring well, without allowing to boil. If sauce is a little too thick add some sherry.
2. When hot, serve over bed of rice.

S E R V E S   6 .

MOULES SAUCE VERTE
Cold Mussels with Green Mayonnaise Sauce

4 qts. freshly gathered mussels,   ¼ *tsp. thyme*
    scrubbed and cleaned   ¼ *lb. butter*
½ *cup shallots or onions,*   1 *tsp. peppercorns*
    finely chopped   6 *sprigs parsley*
1 *cup light dry wine*   12 *lemon wedges*
1 *bay leaf*

NIGHT BEFORE:

1. Put mussels into pail of cold clean water. Occasionally agitate pail. Pour out and refresh water several times.
2. Place shallots, wine, bay leaf, thyme, butter, peppercorns, and parsley into 8-qt. enameled saucepan. Bring mixture to boil for 2 minutes.
3. Add mussels, cover pan tightly, and boil until mussels open (about 5 minutes). While boiling, pick up pan and shake 3 or 4 times to insure even cooking.
4. Discard all mussels that are not opened.
5. Pour liquid into covered plastic container, and freeze for future use as fish stock.
6. Put mussels in covered dish and refrigerate overnight.

JUST BEFORE SERVING:

1. Remove and discard 1 shell from each mussel, leaving meat in other shell.
2. Cover mussels with Sauce Verte (see Striped Bass in Aspic recipe), almost filling each shell.
3. Arrange on bed of lettuce with lemon wedges.

NOTE: If you wish to clean the mussels yourself, be prepared for an hour's work. Mussels *must* be properly cleaned or else bits of sand and seaweed caught in the shells tend to spoil the taste and grind the teeth. With a good stiff scrubbing brush, scrub them under cold running water. Always remove, with a sharp small knife, the little "beard" of seaweed from between the shells.

SERVES 6.

QUENELLES DE BROCHET
Pike Dumplings with Sauce

This dish is a lot of work, but well worth it. Fish in the form of quenelles creates a whole different aura about a very simple basic food. A good French restaurant can well be judged on the quality of its quenelles alone; if they are good, everything else must reflect the kind of care required to make this dish. Try it when you have plenty of time, and try it on the family before serving it to guests.

✎§ *QUENELLES*

¾ cup milk
6 tbsp. plus ½ lb. butter
1¼ tsp. salt
½ tsp. white pepper
¾ cup all-purpose flour

6 whole eggs
¾ lb. boned raw pike (keep
    very cold until used)
2 egg yolks
2 tbsp. heavy cream

✎§ *SAUCE*

2 cups finely minced onion
3 cloves garlic, minced
8 tbsp. butter
½ cup brandy
2½ cups medium-dry sherry

6 tbsp. tomato paste
3 tbsp. chopped parsley
1 tsp. tarragon (dry)
½ tsp. salt
¼ tsp. cayenne pepper

NIGHT BEFORE:

TO MAKE QUENELLES:

1. Bring to boil a combination of the milk, 6 tbsp. butter, ¾ tsp. salt, ¼ tsp. white pepper.

2. When it has just boiled, reduce heat immediately, and add flour. Continue to cook, stirring constantly, until mixture forms ball of paste (called the "panada").

3. Move panada to a mixing bowl, and with electric mixer beat in 3 whole eggs. Continue to mix until panada becomes smooth. Now refrigerate panada and allow it to become well chilled.

4. Cut up fish into small cubes, then run it through blender until it becomes a smooth paste. Transfer paste to another mixing bowl.

5. With electric mixer, beat cold panada into fish paste. Then beat it into remaining 3 whole eggs and 2 egg yolks, 1 cup (½ lb.) chilled butter, ½ tsp. salt, ¼ tsp. white pepper, and heavy cream.

6. When thoroughly mixed, refrigerate and chill for minimum of 2 hours.

7. Just before 2 hours are up, prepare large skillet with about 1½″ simmering (not boiling) salted water. Take out dumpling mixture. With 2 spoons, using about a heaping tbsp. of paste each time, form dumplings. Roll them quickly on lightly floured board, then slip them into simmering water. Poach 10 minutes. Do not allow water to boil.

8. Remove quenelles from water with slotted spoon and drain on absorbent paper. Refrigerate overnight in covered dish. Handle them carefully so that they don't break.

JUST BEFORE SERVING:

1. Remove quenelles from refrigerator and allow to warm up to room temperature on serving platter. This way when sauce is ready you have only to pour it over quenelles and serve.

TO MAKE SAUCE:

2. Sauté onion and garlic in 5 tbsp. butter until onions are golden (about 5 or 6 minutes).

3. Add brandy and cook 5 more minutes.

4. Add sherry, tomato paste, parsley, and tarragon and simmer about 15 minutes.

5. Stir in salt, cayenne, and remaining 3 tbsp. butter.

6. Pour hot sauce over quenelles and serve.

SERVES 6.

SKEWER-BROILED SCALLOPS

For this dish you will need 12–18 small wooden skewers.

2 lbs. sea scallops	½ cup soy sauce
12-oz. can boiled baby onions	1 tsp. grated ginger
1 cup olive oil	1 clove garlic, minced
1 cup dry sherry	½ cup chopped parsley

NIGHT BEFORE:

1. Wash scallops and drain onions. Thread scallops and onions alternately on skewers, leaving enough room on 1 end of each skewer to handle.
2. Mix remaining ingredients thoroughly in shallow flat pan or glass dish. (Rectangular shape is best.)
3. Arrange skewers in marinade and refrigerate overnight. Turn skewers once or twice while marinating to soak scallops and onions completely.

JUST BEFORE SERVING:

Remove skewers from marinade and broil (either over charcoal or under broiler) about 5 minutes, turning to assure broiling on all sides. Serve immediately.

S E R V E S   6 .

STRIPED BASS IN ASPIC
With Special Sauce Verte

1 4-lb. striped bass (cleaned and with head and tail removed)	4 large whole carrots, peeled
	2 stalks celery
¼ lb. butter	½ bay leaf
Salt and pepper	6 bottles clam juice
4 medium-to-large cooking onions, finely chopped (or equivalent weight of shallots)	3 envelopes unflavored gelatin

NIGHT BEFORE:

1. Place bass in fish poacher (or buttered 10"–12" fireproof baking dish, 1½"–2" deep). Butter skin on both sides, and leave remaining piece of butter inside fish.
2. Salt and pepper liberally.
3. Cover fish inside and out with onions, and surround it with carrots, celery, and bay leaf. Pour in 1 or 2 bottles clam juice (enough to almost cover fish).
4. Place in preheated 350° oven, uncovered, 30 minutes.
5. Add remainder of clam juice, cover, and bake 40 minutes or until done. This is evident when meat is uniformly white and permits easy penetration with fork. The fish should not be flaky.
6. Remove fish carefully from poacher and lay on board. Discard celery stalks. Strain remaining juice and refrigerate for later use.
7. Cut carrots into ⅛" slices. Arrange in bottom of 3-qt. ring mold (small individual molds can also be used).
8. Stir 1 envelope of gelatin into ½ cup refrigerated juice, until completely dissolved.
9. Heat almost to boiling, to melt gelatin. Cool. Pour this liquid over carrots in mold. Refrigerate.
10. While this is jelling, carefully separate meat of bass from bones and skin. (Bones are large, easy to remove.)
11. Take mold from refrigerator and quickly arrange meat evenly in mold.
12. Add 2 remaining envelopes of gelatin to rest of cold juice. Use above procedure to dissolve crystals.
13. Heat almost to boiling. Cool.
14. Fill mold to cover all the fish. Refrigerate overnight.

JUST BEFORE SERVING:

1. To unmold, place mold in hot (not boiling) water for 15–20 seconds. Cover mold with serving plate, and quickly turn upside down.
2. At table, either cut into portions or pass plate with knife.

3. Serve with special Sauce Verte.

S E R V E S   6 .

⋙ *SAUCE VERTE*

2 cups mayonnaise
6 drops green food coloring
⅛ tsp. paprika

Juice of one lemon
4 dashes Worcestershire sauce
½ tsp. tarragon leaves

1. Stir ingredients vigorously.
2. Refrigerate before serving. Sauce can also be made the night before and stored in covered container.

VII

EGGS, CRÊPES, BREAD, PIZZA, SAUCES

VII

COLD CURRIED EGGS

6 hard-cooked eggs	¼ tsp. salt
1 tbsp. olive oil	¼ tsp. white pepper
1 tsp. curry powder	1 tbsp. lemon juice
½ cup sherry	¼ cup heavy cream
½ cup mayonnaise	1 tbsp. chopped chives

NIGHT BEFORE:

1. Heat olive oil and curry powder together over low heat a few minutes to make a paste. Do not allow to boil.
2. Add sherry and simmer gently. Reduce volume by about half, then remove from heat.
3. Stir curry sauce into mayonnaise, then add salt, pepper, and lemon juice.
4. Whip heavy cream until soft peaks are formed, then mix whipped cream with mayonnaise curry. Refrigerate sauce overnight in covered dish.
5. Cut hard-cooked eggs in half lengthwise. Carefully remove yolks and force them through a coarse sieve. Store grated yolks separately from whites in refrigerator overnight in covered containers.

JUST BEFORE SERVING:

1. Slice whites into slices about ⅛" thick. Arrange on platter.
2. Spread sauce in layer over whites.
3. Sprinkle first yolks, then chives over top. Serve immediately.

SERVES 6.

DEEP-FRIED CHEESE EGGS

4 tbsp. butter
4 tbsp. flour
1 cup milk
½ tsp. salt
½ tsp. mustard powder
½ cup grated English Cheddar cheese
⅓ cup grated Parmesan cheese

6 eggs
1 additional egg, beaten lightly
1 cup bread crumbs
Fat or oil for deep-frying (quantity depends on type and size of fryer)
¾ cup mayonnaise
¼ cup chopped parsley

NIGHT BEFORE:

1. Melt butter, stir in flour to make thick paste, then stir in milk, a little at a time, followed by salt, mustard, and two cheeses. Remove from heat and allow paste to cool in refrigerator.
2. Boil the 6 eggs 7 minutes. Remove eggs from boiling water and chill.

JUST BEFORE SERVING:

1. Peel and dry boiled eggs.
2. Roll each egg in the cheese paste until well coated.
3. Start frying fat heating to 350°.
4. Now dip coated eggs in beaten egg, then roll in bread crumbs. This operation may have to be done twice for each egg to assure a good coat of bread crumbs on the egg.
5. Deep-fry eggs until they turn golden brown. Remove from fat and drain.
6. Serve immediately with mayonnaise on the side, sprinkled with chopped parsley.

SERVES 6.

OEUFS EN GELÉE WITH CRABMEAT
Eggs in Aspic with Crabmeat

½ cup tiny cooked Icelandic   *2 cooked carrots, thinly sliced*
  shrimps   *1 sprig watercress*
1½ envelopes unflavored gelatin   *6 eggs*
3 cups chicken consommé   *1 cup lump crabmeat*

NIGHT BEFORE:

1. In saucepan, dissolve gelatin in cold consommé until all grains disappear. Bring almost to boil.
2. Allow to cool—but not jell—in refrigerator.
3. Pour ⅛″ liquid into each of 6 small molds (½ to ⅔ cup capacity) or custard cups. Refrigerate.
4. Dip shrimps, one by one, in the cool consommé. Then arrange 3 or 4 shrimps in bottom of each mold. Follow this procedure with carrots and leaves of watercress (2 or 3 leaves per mold). Refrigerate.
5. Soft-boil eggs, which have been at room temperature, 4 minutes in vigorously boiling water. Refrigerate them until quite cold.
6. Gently tap shell of each egg with bottom of teaspoon. *Carefully* flake off shell and slip egg into each mold.
7. Cover egg in each mold with consommé. Refrigerate to set.
8. When set, add layer of crabmeat across top of each mold.
9. Fill to top with remaining consommé.
10. Cover molds with sheets of waxed paper. Refrigerate overnight.

JUST BEFORE SERVING:

1. Dip each mold in hot (not boiling) water 5 seconds.
2. Pass a small knife around inside of molds. Then invert mold and tap bottom sharply with wooden spoon. Unmold onto platter or individual plates.
3. Serve plain or with Sauce Verte (see Striped Bass in Aspic, page 100).

SERVES 6.

NOTE: Red pimiento, tarragon leaves, truffles, black or green olives, or green peppers can be substituted as decorative ingredients. Lobster meat, tuna, shrimps, chicken, or julienne of ham may replace the crabmeat.

POACHED EGGS À LA KING

2 tbsp. finely chopped onion
1 cup finely chopped mush-
    rooms
6 tbsp. butter
4 tbsp. flour
1½ cups heavy cream

½ cup sherry
1½ cups diced cooked chicken
½ tsp. salt
¼ tsp. white pepper
3 English muffins, cut in half
6 eggs

NIGHT BEFORE:

1. Sauté onion and mushrooms in butter about 6 minutes.
2. Stir flour in vigorously, then slowly add cream, a little at a time, to make smooth sauce, stirring all the while.
3. Stir in sherry in same way.
4. Add chicken, salt, and pepper, and stir well. Remove from heat and refrigerate overnight in a covered container.

JUST BEFORE SERVING:

1. Toast English muffins and arrange the 6 toasted halves on serving platter (or 1 each on individual plates). Spread with a little butter.
2. Heat chicken mixture in top of double boiler over simmering water until hot. If it needs a little moisture, add a little chicken stock and stir.
3. Poach eggs.
4. Place 1 poached egg on each ½ muffin, cover all with chicken sauce, and serve immediately.

SERVES 6.

SHIRRED EGGS WITH MUSHROOMS

This recipe requires 6 individual ovenproof au gratin dishes.

½ cup finely chopped onion
2 cups finely minced fresh
* mushrooms*
¼ lb. butter

6 slices white bread
1 dozen eggs
¾ cup cream

NIGHT BEFORE:
1. Sauté onions and mushrooms in half the butter over low heat until mushrooms are soft and most of their liquid is cooked off.
2. Butter the 6 dishes.
3. Trim crusts from bread and toast it.
4. Butter both sides of each piece of toast and lay it in bottom of each dish.
5. Place a layer of sautéed mushrooms and onions over each piece of toast. Let some of the butter they cooked in soak into toast. Refrigerate dishes overnight.

JUST BEFORE SERVING:
1. Preheat oven to 350°.
2. Break 2 eggs over each piece of toast gently, taking care not to break yolks.
3. Add ⅛ cup cream to each dish.
4. Bake 20 minutes (until yolk still soft but white firm) and serve immediately.

SERVES 6.

THIN CRÊPES

1½ tsp. vegetable shortening
1½ cups flour
¾ tsp. salt

4 eggs
2 cups milk
Shortening or butter for cooking

NIGHT BEFORE:

1. Combine all ingredients with rotary beater until smooth.
2. For each crêpe, melt 1 tsp. butter or shortening in crêpe pan or skillet.
3. Fill ladle with 4 tbsp. batter and, holding skillet off fire, ladle batter into skillet. Rotate pan in one quick motion, spreading batter evenly to cover bottom of pan.
4. Cook over medium-high heat until edges of crêpe turn brown. Flip with narrow spatula and cook 20–30 seconds.
5. Remove each crêpe from pan by turning over and tapping into dish.
6. Cover and refrigerate overnight.

JUST BEFORE SERVING:

1. Place 3 tbsp. filling in center of each crêpe. Fold two opposite sides over filling, then roll up carefully.
2. Place rolled crêpe in shallow ovenproof dish.
3. Bake in 400° preheated oven 15 minutes and serve.

SERVES 6.

⋖§ CURRIED SHRIMPS FILLING FOR CRÊPES

36 fresh whole shrimps, uncooked	3 tsp. curry powder
1½ tsp. salt	1 cup clam broth
1 tbsp. dill weed	1 cup heavy cream
1 tbsp. chopped parsley	½ tsp. grated lemon peel
¼ cup butter	5 dashes soy sauce
¼ cup onion, finely chopped	3 drops Tabasco sauce
¼ cup green apple, chopped	¼ tsp. paprika
2½ tbsp. flour	1 tsp. Maggi liquid seasoning (optional)

NIGHT BEFORE:

1. Peel and devein shrimps. (If shrimps are large, cut in half.)
2. Drop into boiling water, adding 1 tsp. salt, dill weed, and parsley. Boil 10 minutes.
3. Remove shrimps and store in sealed container overnight.
4. In butter, slowly sauté onion and apple. Stir in flour and curry powder and cook, without browning, 7 minutes.

5. Slowly add clam broth, cream, and lemon peel. Stir constantly and simmer until well blended.
6. Add soy sauce, Tabasco, ½ tsp. salt, paprika, and Maggi. Stir thoroughly.
7. Store in closed container overnight. Filling is ready for crêpes.

FILLS 6 CRÊPES. CAN ALSO BE USED AS APPETIZER.

COTTAGE CHEESE DESSERT CRÊPE FILLING

1 cup cottage cheese
3 tbsp. sour cream
¼ cup orange marmalade
2 tsp. combined granulated sugar and cinnamon powder (¾–¼)
1 egg well beaten
¼ cup seedless white raisins
¼ cup powdered confectioner's sugar

JUST BEFORE SERVING:

1. Combine cheese, sour cream, and marmalade thoroughly in mixing bowl with fork, breaking up lumps of cottage cheese.
2. Then beat in remaining ingredients until smooth.
3. Place filling in crêpes as directed in recipe for crêpes.
4. When crêpes are removed from oven, dust with powdered sugar before serving.

FILLS 6 CRÊPES.

HAM CRÊPE FILLING

4 tbsp. butter
4 tbsp. flour
1½ cups milk
¼ tsp. salt
⅛ tsp. white pepper
½ cup sour cream
2 cups diced cooked ham
¾ cup chopped cooked mushrooms
1 tbsp. chives, chopped
1 tbsp. chopped parsley

JUST BEFORE SERVING CRÊPES:

1. Melt butter in skillet, stir in flour vigorously until smooth paste is formed. Stir in milk a little at a time, over low heat, and continue to stir until sauce thickens.
2. Season with salt and pepper.
3. Add sour cream, stirring well, keeping heat low.

4. Allow sauce to thicken, but not boil. Now stir in ham, mushrooms, chives, parsley.
5. Place filling in crêpes as directed in recipe for crêpes.

F I L L S 6 C R Ê P E S .

✎§ *CHICKEN AND SPINACH FILLING FOR CRÊPES*

1 lb. diced cooked chicken	*1 tbsp. Maggi liquid seasoning*
12 ozs. chopped cooked spinach	*1 tsp. salt*
(frozen may be substituted)	*½ tsp. pepper*
⅛ lb. butter	*1 tsp. garlic powder*
½ cup flour	*Grated Parmesan cheese*
½ cup chicken broth	*Paprika*

NIGHT BEFORE:

1. Melt butter in top of double boiler. Add flour. Stir until smooth.
2. Add chicken broth, 1 tbsp. at a time, stirring continuously.
3. Season with Maggi, salt, pepper, garlic powder.
4. Mix chicken and spinach into sauce. Cover and refrigerate overnight. Filling is ready for crêpes.

JUST BEFORE SERVING:

Sprinkle filled crêpes with paprika and Parmesan cheese during last five minutes of baking.

F I L L S 6 C R Ê P E S .

GARLIC BREAD

1 18-inch loaf French bread	*¼ cup grated Parmesan cheese*
6 cloves garlic, peeled	*1 tbsp. chopped chives*
¾ cup melted butter	*1 tsp. paprika*

NIGHT BEFORE:

1. Rub outside crust of bread with 2 cut and slightly crushed garlic cloves. Mince other 4 cloves.
2. Split loaf lengthwise, pour butter all over the two cut surfaces. Mix cheese and chives, and sprinkle them equally over buttered surfaces.

3. Now sprinkle on minced garlic, *evenly*, and the paprika.
4. Refrigerate overnight, wrapped in plastic film.

JUST BEFORE SERVING:

1. Preheat oven to 350°.
2. Bake bread 10 minutes, cut into 1″ slices, and serve in basket covered with napkin to keep warm.

S E R V E S   6 .

PIZZA

⋖ *DOUGH*

1 *envelope dry yeast*	½ *tsp. salt*
1 *tsp. sugar*	*Olive oil*
3½ *cups all-purpose flour, sifted*	

⋖ *SAUCE*

1 *medium onion, finely chopped*	1½ *cups tomato paste*
¼ *cup minced green pepper*	½ *tsp. salt*
2 *tbsp. minced pimientos*	¼ *tsp. black pepper*
1 *clove garlic, crushed*	½ *tsp. sugar*
2 *tbsp. olive oil*	½ *tsp. tarragon leaves*

⋖ *TOPPINGS*

¼ *lb. Mozzarella cheese, thinly sliced*	*Canned mushrooms, slices or caps*
Sliced Spanish spicy sausage, or salami	*Grated Parmesan cheese*
Anchovies	*Sliced olives (black or green)*
	4 *eggs*

NIGHT BEFORE:

TO MAKE PIZZA DOUGH:

1. Mix dry yeast and sugar in 1 cup warm (not hot) water, and let stand about 10 minutes.
2. In mixing bowl combine 2 cups sifted flour, salt, and yeast mixture.
3. Now move dough to floured board and knead, adding remaining flour little by little. After all flour is added, continue to knead until dough is smooth. Place ball of dough in bottom of

bowl, cover with towel, and allow to rise in warm draft-free place until doubled in bulk.

4. Return dough to board, and knead again thoroughly. Return to bowl and let rise again about ½ hour.
5. Lightly oil bottom and sides of 12″ pizza pan.
6. Roll out dough on floured board to about ¼″ thickness. Reverse it into oiled pan, then with fingers build up slightly thicker border all around edge. Cover dough with sheet of waxed paper and refrigerate overnight.

TO MAKE SAUCE:

1. Simmer onion, pepper, pimientos, and garlic in olive oil until onions are golden.
2. Stir in remaining sauce ingredients and simmer gently 10 minutes, stirring occasionally.
3. Remove from heat and refrigerate, covered, overnight.

JUST BEFORE SERVING:

1. Stir cold sauce vigorously, then spread evenly over surface of cold, ready pizza dough.
2. Preheat oven to 400°.
3. Arrange slices of Mozzarella cheese evenly over top of sauce.
4. Arrange other topping ingredients over cheese at regular intervals. Any of the toppings can be omitted, according to your taste preferences; the only one really required is the Mozzarella. If you use the eggs, simply open them into little custard cups first. Then slip each egg gently out onto surface of pizza.
5. When all toppings are on, bake at 400° about 20 minutes or until crust at edges is brown and crisp.

MAKES I 12″ PIZZA.

BEEF-TOMATO SPAGHETTI SAUCE

1 *clove garlic, finely chopped*	1 *tsp. sugar*
1 *medium onion, finely chopped*	2 *tsp. salt*
1 *tbsp. olive oil*	1 *tsp. pepper*
1 *lb. ground beef*	1 *lb. canned tomatoes*
1 *small can tomato paste*	2 *tsp. oregano*

NIGHT BEFORE:
1. Sauté garlic and onion in oil over low heat until golden. Add beef to pan and stir until browned. Stir in remaining ingredients.
2. Cook over low heat about 30 minutes, uncovered. Then refrigerate until ready to use.

JUST BEFORE SERVING:
Heat sauce over medium heat until it simmers. Pour over cooked spaghetti and serve.

MAKES ABOUT 4 CUPS.

WHITE CLAM SPAGHETTI SAUCE

*2 cups minced clams (with
their liquid)*
¼ cup olive oil
⅓ cup flour
1 pt. clam juice
2 medium onions, finely chopped

2 cloves garlic, finely chopped
1 green pepper, finely chopped
2 stalks of celery, finely chopped
1 tsp. tarragon
½ tsp. salt
¼ tsp. white pepper

NIGHT BEFORE:
1. Heat oil in saucepan. Add flour, stirring vigorously with wire whisk. Add clam juice, stirring constantly, a little at a time.
2. Now stir in chopped onions, garlic, green pepper, and celery, the tarragon, the salt and pepper. Simmer this sauce over low heat 1 hour, stirring occasionally.
3. When done, remove from heat and refrigerate overnight.

JUST BEFORE SERVING:
Add minced clams to sauce, then heat over medium heat until it simmers. Pour over cooked spaghetti and serve.

MAKES ABOUT 4 CUPS.

MARCHAND DE VIN SAUCE

This is a superior sauce for any red meat. It may be prepared and kept under refrigeration for a couple of days, or frozen for longer. If you freeze it, keep in mind that you must allow enough time for it to thaw when using.

¾ *cup butter*
½ *cup finely chopped onion*
5 *garlic cloves, minced*
⅓ *cup finely chopped shallots*
½ *cup minced cooked ham*
⅓ *cup fresh mushrooms,*
   chopped very fine
2 *tbsp. flour*

½ *tsp. salt*
⅛ *tsp. black pepper*
1 *dash Tabasco sauce*
¾ *cup beef stock*
½ *cup dry red wine*
1 *tbsp. Maggi liquid seasoning*
   (optional)

NIGHT BEFORE:

1. Melt butter in skillet, then sauté onion, garlic, shallots, ham, and mushrooms, stirring occasionally. When onions are golden brown, stir in flour, salt, pepper, Tabasco.
2. Continue to simmer about 10 minutes until well browned.
3. Now add beef stock, wine, and Maggi, simmer over medium low heat 40 minutes.
4. Refrigerate overnight in covered container.

JUST BEFORE SERVING:

Heat thoroughly over boiling water in double boiler. Serve in sauce boat.

MAKES ABOUT 2 CUPS.

VIII

VEGETABLES

VIII

BAKED EGGPLANT

1 *large eggplant*
4 *tbsp. chopped mushrooms*
2 *tbsp. butter*
½ *tsp. salt*
1 *dash pepper*
½ *tbsp. parsley*

1 *dash paprika*
½ *lb. cooked ham, chopped*
3 *hard-boiled eggs, chopped*
8 *anchovies, cut in pieces*
4 *dashes Maggi liquid season-*
   ing (optional)

NIGHT BEFORE:

1. Cook eggplant in salted water 10 minutes, cut off top and remove pulp, leaving enough for a shell. Reserve pulp.
2. In saucepan, fry mushrooms in butter. Add salt, pepper, parsley, paprika. Cool.
3. Chop eggplant pulp. Add to this ham, chopped eggs, and cut up anchovies.
4. Fill eggplant shell with all ingredients.
5. Refrigerate overnight, covered with plastic wrap.

JUST BEFORE SERVING:

1. Sprinkle Maggi into the filled cavity. Bake in 350° oven about 30 minutes or until eggplant is tender.
2. Serve immediately.

SERVES 6.

BAKED GLAZED YAMS

3 *yams*   2 *tbsp. lemon juice*
1 *banana*   ¾ *cup honey*
¼ *cup mixed granulated sugar*
   and cinnamon

NIGHT BEFORE:
1. Cook yams whole in boiling salted water 25 minutes, or until tender but still firm. Drain and allow to cool.
2. Split yams into 6 halves. Scoop meat out with spoon or melon baller.
3. Either mash together thoroughly or run through blender the yam meat, banana, sugar, and cinnamon, and lemon juice. Then return mixture to yam shells.
4. Arrange on ovenproof dish or in baking pan, and refrigerate overnight.

JUST BEFORE SERVING:
1. Preheat oven to 350°.
2. Pour honey over tops of yams, dividing it equally.
3. Bake 15 minutes, basting occasionally, then serve.
                    SERVES 6.

BEETS NELA

2 *lbs. fresh (or canned cooked)*   2 *tsp. meat glaze or* ¼ *cup*
   beets   *beef consommé*
4 *tbsp. butter*   2 *tsp. Maggi liquid seasoning*
4 *tbsp. flour*   *(optional)*
Juice of 1 lemon   ¼ *tsp. salt*
6 *tbsp. powdered sugar*   ½ *cup sour cream*

NIGHT BEFORE:
1. Cut tops from fresh beets, leaving 1″ of stem. Wash beets thoroughly.

2. Half cover them with boiling water in covered saucepan. Cook until tender (1 hour for young beets, 1–2 hours for old beets). Add boiling water as needed.
3. When done, cool them slightly and slip off skins. Retain cooking liquid.
4. Grate beets in coarsest part of grater. If using canned beets, grate them and proceed from here.
5. In double boiler, melt butter and stir in flour to form smooth paste.
6. Stirring constantly, add ½ cup cooking liquid or liquid from can little by little.
7. Add lemon juice. Stir in sugar, glaze or consommé, Maggi, and salt. Stir in sour cream.
8. Add grated beets to sauce. Stir until well blended.
9. Store overnight in covered container in refrigerator.

JUST BEFORE SERVING:
1. Heat thoroughly over simmering water in double boiler.
2. Stir several times until smooth. Serve immediately.

S E R V E S   6 .

CARROT PUDDING

1 *lb. carrots*	1 *tsp. lemon juice*
5 *eggs, separated*	½ *tsp. grated lemon rind*
1 *tsp. salt*	1½ *cups soft bread crumbs*
½ *cup firmly packed brown*	2 *tbsp. melted butter*
sugar	

NIGHT BEFORE:
1. Scrape carrots and grind in blender.
2. Beat egg whites until stiff. Fold in beaten yolks, then salt, sugar, lemon juice, lemon rind, 1 cup bread crumbs, melted butter, and carrots.
3. Refrigerate in covered container overnight.

JUST BEFORE SERVING:

1. Grease and crumb bottom and sides of the top pan of a double boiler and pour in carrot mixture.
2. Cook 1 hour over hot water.
3. Unmold on hot dish and serve with mixed green salad.

SERVES 6.

CAULIFLOWER AND BROCCOLI PIE

1 *medium cauliflower*
1 *bunch broccoli* (note: *There should be equal amounts cauliflower and broccoli*)
Salt
2 *tbsp. butter*
2 *tbsp. flour*

1 *dash nutmeg*
1 *dash Maggi liquid seasoning (optional)*
½ *cup light cream*
2 *egg yolks*
3 *tbsp. melted butter*
4 *tbsp. grated Parmesan cheese*

NIGHT BEFORE:

1. Separate cauliflower florets and boil both vegetables together in salted water until tender. Do not overcook. Reserve cooking water.
2. Brown butter and flour in saucepan. Add to this 1½ cups of water in which you cooked vegetables. Add nutmeg and Maggi.
3. Cook over low heat until mixture thickens.
4. In small bowl, beat cream and egg yolks together. Add to saucepan. Add salt to taste.
5. Place vegetables, drained, overnight in covered bowl in refrigerator.
6. Refrigerate overnight.

JUST BEFORE SERVING:

1. Arrange vegetables in shallow ovenproof dish.
2. Cover with the thick sauce.
3. Pour melted butter over top.
4. Sprinkle evenly with the Parmesan.
5. Bake in 350° oven approximately 30 minutes, until pie bubbles and cheese is melted.

SERVES 6.

CHINESE FRIED RICE

4 cups cooked rice	*¼ cup chopped cooked ham*
8 tbsp. soybean oil	*¼ cup chopped cooked lobster*
4 slightly beaten eggs	*¼ cup cooked green peas*
½ cup chopped fresh scallions	*1 tbsp. molasses*

NIGHT BEFORE:

1. Spread cooked rice in flat roasting pan and heat 20–30 minutes in 250° oven, uncovered, until dry. Stir occasionally.
2. Heat oil in large skillet. Add rice and fry about 7 minutes or until golden, stirring occasionally. Make hollow in center of rice and pour in beaten eggs. Scramble eggs very loosely, then stir with rice until rice is well coated. Add all other ingredients, stir, and cook for 3 or 4 minutes.
3. Refrigerate overnight in covered container.

JUST BEFORE SERVING:

1. Place in shallow casserole and heat in preheated 350° oven 30 minutes. Serve immediately.
2. Or, fill 6–8 custard cups with cold fried rice, packed tight. Then stand cups in shallow pan of simmering water 20 minutes, or until heated through. Unmold individual servings of rice onto warm platter, garnish with parsley, and serve.

SERVES 6.

CREAMED SPINACH RING WITH SHERRY

3 lbs. fresh spinach	*⅓ cup heavy cream*
4 tbsp. butter	*1 cup sliced fresh mushrooms*
⅛ tsp. nutmeg	*¼ cup sherry*
¼ tsp. salt	*3 egg whites*
⅛ tsp. white pepper	

NIGHT BEFORE:

1. Simmer washed fresh spinach in ½ cup water, uncovered, 12

minutes until just softened. Drain on paper towels, then run through finest blade of meat grinder.

2. Return to saucepan and stir in 1 tbsp. butter, nutmeg, salt, pepper, cream.
3. Sauté sliced mushrooms in 2 tbsp. butter 5 minutes over low heat until soft, and stir them into spinach, along with sherry. Refrigerate overnight in covered container.

JUST BEFORE SERVING:

1. Preheat oven to 350°.
2. Butter inside of 1-qt. ring mold. Beat egg whites until they form soft peaks (not too stiff).
3. Fold spinach into egg whites carefully.
4. Set mold in shallow pan of water and bake 45 minutes. Remove from oven, reverse ring onto warm serving platter, and serve.

SERVES 6.

DUCHESS POTATOES

6 *large mature potatoes*	3 *egg yolks*
2 *tsp. salt*	3 *whole eggs*
8 *tbsp. butter (¼ lb.)*	

NIGHT BEFORE:

1. Peel potatoes. Cover them with cold water in ample saucepan. Add salt, bring to boil, boil until potatoes are tender. When a fork goes in easily, they are ready. Remove from water and drain.
2. Put cooked potatoes in large bowl of electric mixer. Beat until they are puréed smooth. Add 6 tbsp. butter, egg yolks, and whole eggs and continue to beat at high speed until mixture is light and fluffy and there are no streaks of yellow from the yolks in evidence.
3. Cover mixing bowl tightly with plastic film and refrigerate overnight.

JUST BEFORE SERVING:

1. Butter a cookie sheet or jelly roll tin with some remaining butter. Melt rest in small pan and have handy.
2. Preheat broiler.
3. Transfer potato mixture into large pastry bag with largest-size decorative tip.
4. Pipe potatoes out onto buttered tin. You can make rosettes, long strips, any pattern you prefer. Sprinkle tops with melted butter, then slip under broiler and brown (watch carefully not to burn).
5. Lift gently with spatula and serve immediately. You can garnish a platter of meat with these, but make sure platter is warm.

SERVES 6.

EGGPLANT PURÉE

3 small eggplants
1 large onion, chopped very fine
3 tsp. salt
½ tsp. pepper
4 tbsp. olive oil

3 tbsp. lemon juice
½ tsp. sugar
1 tsp. brandy or cognac
1 tbsp. chopped chives

NIGHT BEFORE:

1. Cut stems off eggplants and broil eggplants under medium flame. Watch carefully—when cracks begin to appear in skins, remove from broiler and peel.
2. Put peeled eggplants through food mill or mash them with fork in mixing bowl. Beat in onion, salt, pepper, olive oil, lemon juice, sugar, and cognac.
3. Store in mixing bowl in refrigerator overnight, covered.

JUST BEFORE SERVING:

Turn out onto serving platter, sprinkle with chopped chives, and serve.

SERVES 6.

BASIC FLORENTINE SPINACH BED

Among the dishes that best lend themselves to advance preparation are "Florentine" dishes. Traditionally, "Florentine" in the name of a dish means "on a bed of spinach." In the recipes that follow, first is the preparation of the basic spinach bed, which can be entirely done the night before. After that come ingredients and sauces to serve on the spinach bed.

2 lbs. fresh spinach	1 tsp. salt
4 tbsp. butter	½ tsp. pepper
½ cup finely chopped onion	2 tsp. sugar
2 tbsp. flour	½ tsp. Maggi liquid seasoning
1 cup hot heavy cream (not boiled)	(optional)

NIGHT BEFORE:

1. Pick over fresh spinach and cut away all thick stems and roots. Then wash thoroughly in cold water in a colander.

2. Set 1 qt. (4 cups) water to boiling rapidly in heavy enameled saucepan. Put washed spinach in boiling water and reduce heat to medium. Simmer spinach, covered, for 15–20 minutes, until tender. Length of cooking time depends on age of spinach. Young spinach takes less time than more mature.

3. Remove spinach from heat and drain off (by shaking in a sieve) most of water. Do not dry it out completely.

4. Purée spinach in blender, or with spinach chopper in wooden bowl, or with food mill, finest blade.

5. Melt butter in skillet and sauté chopped onion until golden and transparent.

6. Stir in flour and blend thoroughly with butter in pan.

7. Add hot cream and stir until smooth.

8. Add puréed spinach to pan and stir well with onions and cream. Add salt, pepper, sugar, and Maggi, stir, and remove from heat after 5 minutes.

9. Butter inside of 1½-qt. baking dish, turn spinach purée into it. Let cool, then stretch a plastic wrap or foil across the top to cover tightly and refrigerate.

The "Florentine" base is now ready for the addition of other ingredients or sauces, below.

⋙ FILETS OF FLOUNDER FLORENTINE

2 lbs. filets of flounder	2 cups hot milk
1 cup white wine	½ tsp. salt
5 tbsp. butter	¼ tsp. pepper
4 tbsp. flour	

NIGHT BEFORE:

1. Lay filets in a large shallow skillet. Add wine and 1 cup water and dot filets with 1 tbsp. butter.
2. Place skillet over high heat and watch carefully until liquid boils. Then reduce heat to simmer gently 8 minutes, uncovered.
3. Turn off heat. Very carefully remove filets with spatula onto paper towels spread out for draining. Retain poaching liquid in separate container for use in sauce.
4. Refrigerate filets overnight in covered container.

JUST BEFORE SERVING:

1. Make layer of filets over top of spinach bed.
2. Preheat oven to 400°.
3. Melt 4 tbsp. butter in top of double boiler over simmering water. Add flour and blend thoroughly until smooth.
4. Slowly add milk, stirring constantly to keep sauce smooth. Add the poaching liquid, salt and pepper, and stir until smooth.
5. Pour sauce over fish filets on spinach.
6. Bake 20 minutes, or until well heated through. Or, put dish under broiler for just long enough to brown top of sauce just before serving. If you do this, never take your eyes off surface of dish while broiling; it can take less than a minute.

SERVES 6.

⋙ EGGS FLORENTINE

1 dozen eggs	½ tsp. salt
4 tbsp. butter	¼ tsp. pepper
4 tbsp. flour	1 cup grated Parmesan cheese
2 cups hot milk	½ tsp. Worcestershire sauce

NIGHT BEFORE:

1. Poach eggs, handling them very gently, leaving yolks runny and whites firm.
2. Drain poached eggs on paper towels and refrigerate overnight, covered.

JUST BEFORE SERVING:

1. Make layer of poached eggs on surface of spinach bed.
2. Preheat oven to 400°.
3. Melt butter in top of double boiler over simmering water. Add flour and blend thoroughly until smooth.
4. Slowly add milk, stirring constantly to keep smooth. Now add salt, pepper, grated cheese, and Worcestershire. Keep stirring until cheese has melted into sauce.
5. Pour sauce over eggs in baking dish and bake 20 minutes. Or, as in the Filets of Flounder Florentine recipe, you can put dish under the broiler just before serving to brown the top.

SERVES 6.

⋙ MUSHROOMS FLORENTINE

1 ½-oz. package European dried mushrooms	2 cups hot milk
	½ tsp. salt
1 dozen large fresh mushrooms	¼ tsp. pepper
6 tbsp. butter	¼ tsp. Maggi liquid seasoning
4 tbsp. flour	(optional)

NIGHT BEFORE:

1. Soak dried mushrooms for 1 hr. in 1½ cups boiling hot water (off heat).
2. While they are soaking, wash fresh mushrooms, and carefully remove stems from caps.
3. Mince stems fine. Remove soaking mushrooms from liquid. Remove liquid to saucepan. Now mince soaked mushrooms and mix with minced stems.
4. In saucepan of reserved liquid, simmer mushroom caps, with 1 tbsp. butter added, 5 minutes. Remove caps, drain, and refrigerate overnight. Again, reserve liquid.
5. In another tbsp. butter, sauté minced stems and dried mush-

rooms about 5 minutes, then refrigerate overnight in covered container.

JUST BEFORE SERVING:

1. Arrange mushroom caps on bed of spinach.
2. Preheat oven to 400°.
3. Melt butter in top of double boiler over simmering water. Add flour and blend thoroughly until smooth.
4. Slowly add milk, stirring constantly to keep smooth. Now add salt, pepper, Maggi, mushroom liquid, and minced mushrooms. Keep stirring another minute or two.
5. Pour sauce over mushroom caps on spinach bed and bake 20 minutes.
6. Serve immediately. Or, you can toast top of dish under broiler just before serving, as in recipe for Filets of Flounder Florentine.

SERVES 6.

NOTE: Other Florentine dishes can be made with almost any meat, fish, or crustaceans. The basic procedures are always the same, using some essence of the meat or fish in the cream sauce to give it added taste. The prepared cooked spinach bed will keep several days in the refrigerator if tightly covered, or it can be frozen for longer periods, but in that case you have to allow a couple of hours for it to thaw to room temperature before using.

HAGYMAS PAPRIKAS KRUMPLI
Boiled Paprika Potatoes

6 *medium new potatoes*   1 tsp. paprika
1 *large onion, finely chopped*   ¼ tsp. salt
5 *tbsp. butter*

NIGHT BEFORE:

1. Wash potatoes. Drop into boiling salted water and boil rapidly 20–30 minutes, or until tender (depending on size).
2. Allow to cool, then peel and slice.
3. Refrigerate slices overnight in covered container.

JUST BEFORE SERVING:

1. In heavy skillet, sauté onions in butter until golden. Add paprika and let it dissolve in butter. Stir in potatoes and let them heat through without frying (use very low flame).
2. Sprinkle with salt and serve hot.

SERVES 6.

QUICK FRIED RICE

½ lb. bacon, cubed
1 onion, chopped
2 eggs, lightly beaten
2 tbsp. soy sauce
½ tsp. salt

½ tsp. pepper
4 cups cold cooked short-grain rice
5 dashes Maggi liquid seasoning (optional)

NIGHT BEFORE:

1. Cook bacon in frying pan. Add onion and eggs, frying slightly on both sides.
2. Add remaining ingredients (including 3 dashes Maggi), stirring constantly. Mix well. Cook 3–4 minutes.
3. Cool. Refrigerate overnight in covered container.

JUST BEFORE SERVING:

1. Place rice in covered double boiler over boiling water.
2. Let steam 15–20 minutes.
3. Stir and add 2 dashes Maggi. Serve hot.

SERVES 6.

RATATOUILLE NIÇOISE

3 small zucchini
4 medium tomatoes
1 small onion, thinly sliced
¼ cup olive oil
2 sweet red peppers
1 clove garlic, minced very fine

½ tsp. sugar
¼ tsp. white pepper
⅛ tsp. mustard powder
¼ tsp. salt
¼ cup chopped parsley

NIGHT BEFORE:

1. Slice zucchini into very thin slices (about ⅛"). Peel tomatoes by dipping into boiling water a moment, then removing only thin outer skin. Cut tomatoes into small cubes.
2. Simmer onion in olive oil until golden. Add tomatoes, stir for a moment, then add all remaining ingredients except parsley.
3. Cover and simmer about 3 minutes.
4. Remove cover and continue to cook over medium low heat until liquids have evaporated completely. Watch carefully— do not allow to burn.
5. Remove from heat and refrigerate, covered, overnight.

JUST BEFORE SERVING:

Hot: Reheat in top of double boiler and serve as vegetable. Sprinkle with parsley before serving.

Cold: Simply remove from refrigerator and serve, sprinkled with parsley.

SERVES 6.

SCALLOPED POTATOES AU GRATIN

6 medium mature potatoes
½ tsp. salt
¼ tsp. white pepper
1–2 cups milk or half and half
(amount needed depends on

quality of potatoes and size of
baking dish used)
2 tbsp. butter
½ cup grated Parmesan cheese

NIGHT BEFORE:

1. Peel potatoes. Slice carefully, paper-thin (no thicker than 3/16". If you have a meat slicing machine, use it for this. setting slicer for ⅛". This is the most important operation of the recipe, and uniformity of slices is highly desirable).
2. Separate slices from each other and arrange in layers in oven-proof baking dish. Season each layer with a little salt and pepper before starting next.
3. Fill dish with milk level with top layer of potatoes. Dot with butter evenly over surface.

4. Bake in 250° oven 1½ hours. Refrigerate, covered, overnight.

JUST BEFORE SERVING:

1. Preheat oven to 400°.
2. Moisten potatoes with about ¼ cup milk sprinkled on top and bake 20 minutes.
3. Now sprinkle cheese over top, put under broiler just long enough to melt cheese and brown it a little. Serve directly from baking dish.

SERVES 6.

STRING BEANS À LA FRANÇAISE

1½ lbs. fresh string beans	*⅓ tsp. fresh pepper*
3 medium onions, thinly sliced	*2 tbsp. chopped parsley*
3 tbsp. butter	*4 tbsp. red wine vinegar*
1½ tsp. salt	

NIGHT BEFORE:

1. Remove strings from beans. Split and wash them.
2. Drop into boiling salted water and boil rapidly 10 minutes. Remove from water, drain, and refrigerate overnight wrapped in a towel.
3. Slice onions for tomorrow.

JUST BEFORE SERVING:

1. This can be done in minutes while your guests are finishing the first course: Sauté sliced onions in butter until golden brown.
2. Toss in beans, salt, and pepper. Sauté until beans are just barely getting a little browned.
3. Transfer to warm vegetable dish, sprinkle with parsley, add vinegar, toss like a salad, and serve immediately.

SERVES 6.

STUFFED BAKED TOMATOES

6 *large tomatoes*   ⅛ *tsp. pepper*
½ *cup chopped scallions*   1 *tsp. Maggi liquid seasoning*
¼ *lb. butter*   (*optional*)
2 *cloves garlic, chopped*   4 *slices white bread, crusts*
½ *lb. ground cooked ham*   *trimmed*
¼ *tsp. salt*   ½ *cup bread crumbs*

NIGHT BEFORE:

1. Slice off tops of tomatoes. Scoop out insides with melon baller (leaving firm enough shell so tomatoes don't collapse).
2. Soften scallions in all but 2 tbsp. butter over medium heat. Add garlic, ham, tomato pulp, salt, pepper, Maggi. Wet bread, squeeze it, and mash into mixture.
3. Stuff mixture into tomato shells, cover open tops with bread crumbs, dot with butter, and refrigerate overnight in broiler pan.

JUST BEFORE SERVING:

1. Preheat oven to 350°.
2. Bake 10 minutes, serve immediately.

SERVES 6.

IX

SALADS AND SALAD
DRESSINGS

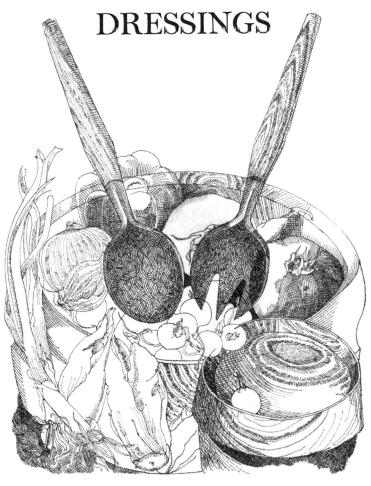

IX

CHICKEN-AVOCADO SALAD

3 *cups cubed cooked chicken meat*
3 *large ripe avocados, peeled, pitted, and sliced*
⅓ *cup slivered white almonds*
¼ *tsp. salt*
¼ *tsp. pepper*

1 *tsp. lemon juice*
3 *hard-boiled eggs, cut in quarters*
¼ *cup chopped parsley*
Mayonnaise
Lettuce leaves

NIGHT BEFORE:

1. Toss gently in a deep bowl the chicken meat, slices of avocado, and almonds, season with salt and pepper and lemon juice.
2. Arrange platter with bed of lettuce leaves. Make mound of avocado chicken-mixture in center. Surround with egg quarters, sprinkle chopped parsley over all.
3. Make a circle of mayonnaise around outside of circle of egg quarters. Refrigerate overnight.

JUST BEFORE SERVING:

Just remove from refrigerator and serve!

S E R V E S   6 .

CRABMEAT AND BEAN SPROUT SALAD

1 cup mayonnaise
3 tbsp. soy sauce
2 tbsp. Maggi liquid seasoning
  (optional)
3 tbsp. curry powder
2 tbsp. lemon juice
1 lb. crabmeat
1-lb. can bean sprouts

1 cup celery, diced
3 tbsp. green onions, minced
½ cup toasted almonds,
  slivered
Salt
Pepper
Boston lettuce
Paprika

NIGHT BEFORE:

1. Mix mayonnaise, soy sauce, Maggi, curry powder, and lemon juice. Refrigerate overnight in tightly covered jar or plastic container.

JUST BEFORE SERVING:

1. Pick over crabmeat.
2. Mix crabmeat with bean sprouts, celery, green onions, and ⅓ cup almonds.
3. Stir dressing and add salt and pepper to taste. Add a dash of Maggi if you wish richer flavor.
4. Mix salad and dressing together thoroughly.
5. Arrange on beds of lettuce, sprinkle with remaining almonds and paprika, and serve.

SERVES 6–8.

CUCUMBER CREAM SALAD

3 medium-to-large cucumbers
½ pt. sour cream
1 tbsp. lemon juice

1 tbsp. chopped chives (frozen
  will do)
⅛ tsp. paprika

NIGHT BEFORE:

1. Peel cucumbers with potato peeler (don't use a knife, it takes too much skin off). Then slice cucumbers very, very thinly.

By far the best way to do this is with a standing rectangular grater, the kind that has four different working surfaces. Use the side with the single, wide cutting slot. All you have to do is rub the cucumber rapidly back and forth over this slot. The perfectly thin slices fall in the middle, and you can do the three cucumbers in about 5 minutes.

2. In glass or ceramic bowl (not a wooden one) stir vigorously sour cream, lemon juice, chives, and paprika until well blended with a runny texture.

3. Refrigerate cream mixture and sliced cucumbers separately overnight, covered.

JUST BEFORE SERVING:

1. Add cucumbers to cream mixture and toss thoroughly until all slices are well coated with dressing.

2. Serve on salad plates. This salad should never be served on same plate with anything else because dressing runs.

S E R V E S   6 .

EGGPLANT SALAD
From South America

2 medium eggplants   2 tsp. minced onion
2 tbsp. lemon juice   1 cup diced celery
¼ tsp. salt   ¾ cup chopped walnuts
¼ tsp. paprika   Romaine lettuce
⅛ tsp. white pepper   3 hard-cooked eggs, sliced
3 tsp. wine vinegar   ½ cup pitted black olives
3 drops onion juice   ½ cup mayonnaise
6 tbsp. olive oil   Paprika

NIGHT BEFORE:

1. Peel eggplants. Cut into cubes.

2. Simmer eggplant cubes in boiling salted water with 1 tsp. lemon juice until tender. Drain and refrigerate overnight in covered container.

3. Beat together the salt, paprika, white pepper, vinegar, and

onion juice, remaining lemon juice, and olive oil. Blend thoroughly. Add minced onion and celery to dressing and refrigerate overnight in tightly sealed jar or container.

JUST BEFORE SERVING:

1. Mix walnuts and eggplant.
2. Stir dressing thoroughly and add to eggplant mixture.
3. Arrange salad on Romaine lettuce beds garnished with slices of egg and olives.
4. Top each serving with heaping spoonful of mayonnaise sprinkled with paprika, and serve.

SERVES 6.

FRUIT AND MINT SALAD

6 *navel oranges*
3 *cups canned grapefruit sections*
2 *cans mandarin oranges*
1 *large bunch fresh mint, chopped*

½ *cup olive oil*
4 *tbsp. lemon juice*
3 *tbsp. cognac*
Boston lettuce
1 *bunch watercress*

NIGHT BEFORE:

1. Peel oranges, removing all white inner skin. Slice, discarding ends.
2. Drain grapefruit and mandarin oranges. Mix with oranges and chopped mint and refrigerate overnight in covered container.

JUST BEFORE SERVING:

1. Make dressing of olive oil, lemon juice, and cognac. Change proportions according to taste. Pour over fruit and chill well.
2. Serve on lettuce with watercress.

SERVES 6.

GERMAN BEAN SALAD

3 lbs. canned baby lima beans
1 medium onion, thinly sliced
1 cup sour cream
3 tbsp. wine vinegar
2 tbsp. granulated sugar
1 tsp. horseradish

3 tsp. salt
½ tsp. freshly ground pepper
1 tsp. Maggi liquid seasoning
   (optional)
¼ cup parsley, chopped

NIGHT BEFORE:
1. Drain beans thoroughly. Add onion and toss.
2. Beat together sour cream, vinegar, sugar, horseradish, salt, and pepper. Add to beans and onions.
3. Refrigerate in covered container overnight.

JUST BEFORE SERVING:
1. Toss salad lightly. Add Maggi if desired.
2. Serve topped with chopped parsley.

SERVES 6.

MUSHROOM SALAD

½ cup olive oil
4 tbsp. red vinegar
4 tbsp. lemon juice
½ tsp. salt

¼ tsp. fresh ground black
   pepper
12 large fresh mushrooms
1 bunch watercress
½ cup fresh chopped chives

NIGHT BEFORE:
1. Make dressing by thoroughly mixing oil, vinegar, lemon juice, salt, and pepper.
2. Wash, then slice mushrooms paper-thin. Soak slices in dressing, refrigerated, overnight.

JUST BEFORE SERVING:
1. Transfer mushrooms and dressing to salad bowl. Wash and drain watercress and add to bowl.

2. Toss salad vigorously.
3. Sprinkle chives over top and serve.

SERVES 6.

POTATO SALAD IN SOUR CREAM DRESSING

2 *lbs. potatoes*	½ *tsp. salt*
3 *stalks celery*	⅛ *tsp. white pepper*
1 *tbsp. powdered sugar*	6 *slices ham, cut into julienne*
1 *tbsp. lemon juice*	*strips*
1 *cup sour cream*	¼ *cup chopped fresh chives*
2 *tbsp. vinegar*	

NIGHT BEFORE:

1. Boil potatoes, unpeeled, in enough water to cover until cooked but still firm. To test, a fork should go into largest potato with gentle pressure without strong resistance. Remove potatoes from heat and refrigerate until cold.
2. Now peel potatoes and cut into julienne strips (first into ¼" thick slices, then into strips lengthwise). Handle gently from now on so as not to break them up.
3. Cut celery stalks into 2" lengths, then julienne strips. Gently mix celery and potatoes.
4. Dissolve sugar in lemon juice. Whisk together sour cream, lemon juice, vinegar, salt, and pepper. Pour dressing over potato salad in serving bowl and mix gently. Sprinkle top of salad with julienne strips of ham and chopped chives. Refrigerate overnight, loosely covered with plastic wrap.

JUST BEFORE SERVING:

Your salad stands ready as is.

SERVES 6.

RED CABBAGE SALAD

1 medium head red cabbage   1 pt. heavy cream
½ cup tarragon vinegar   3 tsp. lemon juice
¼ tsp. salt   2 tbsp. leek, chopped (onion
¼ tsp. pepper   may be substituted)
6 egg yolks, hard-cooked   1 bunch radishes, sliced
                                 3 cucumbers, minced

NIGHT BEFORE:

1. Discard outer leaves of cabbage. Wash cabbage and cut into julienne strips.
2. Drop cabbage into boiling salted water a few seconds and remove.
3. Drain cabbage by placing in colander and shaking. Remove to mixing bowl. Mix vinegar with salt and pepper. Pour this over cabbage and refrigerate 1½ hours. Turn often.
4. Hard-boil eggs. Refrigerate overnight.
5. Pour off marinade from cabbage and refrigerate cabbage in covered container.

JUST BEFORE SERVING:

1. Peel eggs and scoop out yolks. Force yolks through sieve.
2. Mix yolks with cream and lemon juice. Add leek and cabbage. Mix well. Salt and pepper to taste.
3. Slice radishes and mince cucumbers.
4. Serve salad topped with radish-cucumber combination.

SERVES 6.

SALAD ESPAGÑOLE
Spanish Salad

5 *medium-sized potatoes*
French Garlic Dressing
2 *lbs. fresh peas*
2 *small onions, finely chopped*
4 *eggs, hard-boiled and chopped*
½ *lb. cooked ham or prosciutto, diced*
4 *tbsp. paprika*

2 *cups mayonnaise*
Salt
Freshly ground black pepper
3 *dashes Maggi liquid seasoning (optional)*
1 *cup fresh parsley, chopped*
Boston lettuce

NIGHT BEFORE:

1. Cook potatoes in their skins in boiling salted water 25 minutes or until tender.
2. Drain and cool. Remove skins.
3. Dice potatoes and marinate in a little French Garlic Dressing (*see* page 143). Let stand until cool.
4. Cook peas 10 minutes or until tender. Drain and cool.
5. Combine potatoes, onions, eggs, ham, peas, and 3 tbsp. paprika.
6. Refrigerate overnight in covered container.

JUST BEFORE SERVING:

1. Mix ingredients with mayonnaise until you achieve desired consistency.
2. Salt and pepper to taste. Sprinkle with Maggi and toss.
3. Top with chopped parsley and 1 tbsp. paprika just before serving.
4. Serve chilled on beds of Boston lettuce.

SERVES 6 AS A MAIN COURSE.

SALADE RUSSE

This is a salad comprised of many varieties of fresh vegetables, with
a mayonnaise sauce.

½ lb. string beans	*1 tomato*
1 lb. fresh peas	*½ cucumber*
2 medium beets	*2 large mushrooms*
2 small potatoes	*2 dashes Maggi liquid season-*
1 avocado	*ing (optional)*
3 medium carrots	*2 eggs, hard-boiled*
1 apple	*1 bunch parsley*
1 small onion	*1 small square of pimiento*

NIGHT BEFORE:

1. Steam or boil (we recommend steaming) beans, peas, beets,
   carrots, and potatoes—each separately. Dice potatoes and
   beets.
2. Peel and pit avocado, cut into strips.
3. Cut carrots into little slices. Core and peel apple, cut into small
   squares. Slice tomato.
4. Chop onion finely (do not cook). Peel and dice cucumber.
   Steam and slice mushrooms.
5. Refrigerate all overnight.

JUST BEFORE SERVING:

1. Toss in large bowl. Add Maggi.
2. Garnish with slices of hard-boiled egg, parsley and pimiento.
3. Serve with Mayonnaise Sauce.

S E R V E S   6 – 8 .

~§ *MAYONNAISE SAUCE*

1 cup mayonnaise	*Salt and pepper to taste*
Juice 1 lemon	

Blend evenly and serve with salad.

SCANDINAVIAN SALAD

2 salted herring filets
2 cups apples, peeled and diced
2 cups boiled potatoes, peeled
and diced
½ cup onions, coarsely chopped
1 cup cucumbers, peeled and
diced

2 tbsp. brown sugar
½ cup lemon juice
¼ tsp. pepper
1 cup sour cream (½ pt.)
¼ cup fresh chopped chives

NIGHT BEFORE:

1. Soak herring in cold fresh water several hours (this can be done on the "morning before").
2. Dice herring (remove any big bones). Toss with prepared apples, potatoes, onions, cucumbers.
3. Rub sugar, lemon juice, and pepper together in shallow wooden bowl to make dressing. Pour dressing over salad and toss again.
4. Refrigerate overnight, loosely covered with plastic wrap.

JUST BEFORE SERVING:

1. Add sour cream to bowl and toss, mixing well.
2. Sprinkle chopped chives over top and serve.

SERVES 6.

SWEET-AND-SOUR SALAD

2 large red onions
½ cup red vinegar
2 large oranges
1-lb. can sliced pineapple
5 tbsp. olive oil
1 tbsp. orange juice

1 tbsp. lemon juice
1 tbsp. brown sugar
½ tsp. salt
¼ tsp. pepper
Lettuce

NIGHT BEFORE:

1. Peel onions and slice thinly (⅛″ slices). Marinate onion slices 3 hours in vinegar.
2. Peel and slice oranges, drain pineapple slices.

3. Store fruit and onion slices overnight in refrigerator in separate, tightly covered containers.
4. To make dressing: Mix olive oil, orange and lemon juices. Crush brown sugar in liquid and dissolve. Add salt and pepper.

JUST BEFORE SERVING:

1. Arrange orange, pineapple, and onion slices alternating on bed of lettuce on platter.
2. Shake or mix dressing vigorously, pour over top. Serve.

SERVES 6.

ALMOND-CUCUMBER DRESSING

¼ cup cucumbers, unpeeled but finely chopped
4 tbsp. toasted almonds, slivered and blanched
½ tsp. curry powder
¾ cup olive oil
¼ cup lemon juice

1 tsp. fresh dill (dill weed may be substituted)
¾ tsp. salt
½ tsp. freshly ground black pepper
½ tsp. garlic powder

NIGHT BEFORE:

1. In large bowl, mix ingredients well.
2. Refrigerate in covered container overnight.

JUST BEFORE SERVING:

Stir briskly. Serve over seafood, meat, or vegetable salads.

MAKES ABOUT 1½ CUPS.

CAVIAR DRESSING

1-oz. jar black caviar
¼ cup mayonnaise
½ cup sour cream
4 tsp. chili sauce
1 tsp. lemon juice

1 tsp. onion, minced
¼ tsp. Worcestershire sauce
⅛ tsp. seasoned salt
1 dash Tabasco sauce

NIGHT BEFORE:

1. In large bowl, combine ingredients thoroughly.
2. Refrigerate overnight in covered container.

JUST BEFORE SERVING:

Stir briskly. Serve over Belgian endive or wedges of head lettuce.

MAKES I CUP.

CREAM CHEESE SALAD DRESSING

This is a blender dressing that can be made ahead and stored in a jar.

1 6-oz. package cream cheese,
softened at room temperature
½ tsp. curry powder
1 small onion (1¼" diameter)
1 tsp. salt
¼ tsp. freshly ground black
pepper

1 tbsp. fresh chopped parsley
1 tbsp. fresh (or frozen)
chopped chives
⅓ cup olive oil
2 tbsp. vinegar

NIGHT BEFORE:

1. Place all ingredients in blender jar and blend until smooth.
2. Transfer to covered jar and refrigerate. (Do not use narrow-necked bottle.)

JUST BEFORE SERVING:

Shake vigorously before opening jar. Pour dressing over salad and toss.

MAKES ABOUT I CUP.

FRENCH GARLIC DRESSING

2 tsp. salt
½ tsp. freshly ground black
pepper
½ tsp. powdered mustard
1 clove garlic
2 cups olive oil

3 tbsp. lemon juice
1 egg white
½ cup wine vinegar
2 dashes Maggi liquid season-
ing (optional)

NIGHT BEFORE:
1. Mix ingredients together in large bowl with hand beater.
2. Refrigerate overnight in tightly sealed jar.

JUST BEFORE SERVING:
Shake jar vigorously, pour dressing over salad and serve.

MAKES 3 CUPS.

GREEN GODDESS DRESSING

1 2-oz. can (or 1¾″ tube)
   anchovy paste
1 cup sour cream
1 cup mayonnaise
3 tbsp. chopped chives (or
   frozen chives, if necessary)
1 tbsp. lemon juice

3 tbsp. tarragon vinegar
½ cup parsley, chopped
½ tsp. salt
½ tsp. freshly ground pepper
1 garlic clove, crushed
1 tbsp. powdered sugar

NIGHT BEFORE:
1. Place ingredients in blender jar and blend 20 seconds at high speed. Or beat thoroughly with rotary beater.
2. Refrigerate in tightly sealed jar overnight.

JUST BEFORE SERVING:
Blend a few seconds in blender, and serve over salad.

MAKES ABOUT 3 CUPS.

HARD-BOILED EGG MAYONNAISE DRESSING
For Seafood Cocktails and Salads

2 hard-boiled eggs
1 cup mayonnaise
½ tsp. salt
¼ tsp. black pepper
½ tsp. Worcestershire sauce

½ tsp. Maggi liquid seasoning
   (optional)
½ tsp. lemon juice
2 tbsp. sour cream
1 tbsp. parsley

NIGHT BEFORE:
1. Shell hard-boiled eggs. Rub them through coarsest sieve into bowl.
2. Briskly mix in all remaining ingredients and refrigerate.

JUST BEFORE SERVING:

1. Dressing should remain chilled until last minute. Spoon over individual servings of shrimp, crabmeat, or lobster cocktails.
2. Or, serve in separate small cup as dip. Or, spoon over salad and toss.

MAKES 2 CUPS.

LEMON SALAD DRESSING

¼ cup chives or green onion
sprouts
1½ tsp. granulated sugar
¼ tsp. freshly ground pepper
¼ tsp. salt

2 tbsp. olive oil
Juice of 2 lemons
1 drop Maggi liquid seasoning
(optional)

NIGHT BEFORE:

1. Put chives, sugar, pepper, and salt in small wooden bowl and crush to a paste, slowly adding olive oil and lemon juice alternately.
2. Stir vigorously until mixture is completely smooth.
3. Add Maggi for stronger taste (or dill or other herb if preferred).
4. Cover bowl with plastic wrap and store in refrigerator overnight.

JUST BEFORE SERVING:

Stir vigorously. Taste and add seasonings if necessary, and serve.

MAKES ABOUT I CUP.

ROQUEFORT DRESSING

6 tbsp. olive oil (use best avail-
able French or Italian oil)
2 tbsp. tarragon or red wine
vinegar
1 tbsp. lemon juice
1 tsp. powdered sugar

1 tsp. salt
1 tsp. freshly ground black
pepper
1½ ozs. real Roquefort cheese
(half of a standard 3-oz.
wedge)
1 tsp. dried tarragon

NIGHT BEFORE:

1. In shallow bowl mix oil, vinegar, lemon juice, sugar, salt, and pepper.
2. With fork, mash Roquefort into liquid, leaving very small crumbs of cheese. (If you like a very strong Roquefort taste, you can use more cheese and leave bigger pieces in the dressing.)
3. Stir in tarragon. Refrigerate overnight in tightly covered bottle or jar.

JUST BEFORE SERVING:

1. Make sure your salad leaves have been well washed, and drained almost completely dry.
2. Just before serving salad, shake bottle of dressing vigorously. Pour over salad and toss thoroughly until all leaves are coated and cheese bits well scattered through salad.

MAKES ABOUT ⅔ CUP — ENOUGH
FOR A SALAD FOR 6.

TROPICAL SALAD DRESSING

This dressing is good for salads that contain fruits, cottage cheese, gelatins of various flavors.

½ cup French olive oil	1 tsp. brown sugar
½ cup pineapple juice	1 ripe banana
1 tsp. lemon juice	¼ orange, peeled and pitted

NIGHT BEFORE:

Blend all ingredients in blender at high speed 90 seconds until smooth. Store in refrigerator in capped jar or bottle.

JUST BEFORE SERVING:

Shake container well, and pour dressing over salad. If you don't use all of it, keep under refrigeration for further use.

MAKES ABOUT 1½ CUPS.

X

BAKED DESSERTS

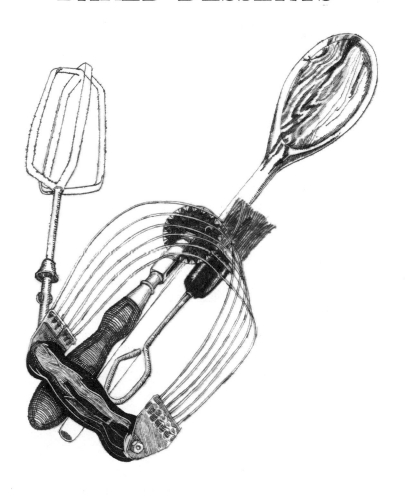

X

ALMOND SUGAR STICKS

½ lb. butter (2 sticks)
5 tbsp. granulated sugar
1 tbsp. grated orange rind
2 cups sifted flour

1 cup ground white almonds
1 tsp. almond extract
½ cup confectioners powdered
sugar

NIGHT BEFORE:

1. With electric mixer cream together butter, granulated sugar, and orange rind.
2. Continue mixing and add flour, ground almonds, and almond extract.
3. Roll dough into ball, wrap in waxed paper, and refrigerate over night.

JUST BEFORE SERVING:

1. Take out dough and knead with hands to warm up.
2. Roll into 3" long, finger-thick sticks.
3. Preheat oven to 300°.
4. Place sticks on greased cookie sheet and bake 40 minutes.
5. Remove from oven and take cookies off sheet with spatula, place sticks crosswise on cooling rack. Cool 10 minutes, then roll in confectioners sugar and serve.

MAKES ABOUT 2 DOZ. STICKS.

BABKA AU RHUM

¼ cup half and half (milk
and cream)
1 envelope dry yeast
¾ cup sugar
¼ cup melted butter (clarified)
3 eggs

2½ cups sifted flour
⅛ tsp. salt
½ cup white raisins
¼ cup white slivered almonds
½ cup chocolate chips
2 tbsp. light rum

NIGHT BEFORE:

1. Preheat oven to 375°. Sprinkle yeast over lukewarm ¼ cup water and ¼ cup half & half, then add ¼ tsp. sugar and set aside until it bubbles from fermentation.

2. Mix butter, ¼ cup sugar, eggs, flour and salt, in large bowl. Combine mixture with yeast mixture, cover bowl with damp cloth, allow to rise in warm, draft-free place until it doubles in bulk (about 1½ hours).

3. Now remove to lightly floured board and knead for 2 or 3 minutes. Work in raisins, almonds, and finally chocolate chips. Then place in greased 2-qt. kuglehof pan or tall angel-food mold. Allow to rise again until bulk is doubled.

4. Bake 30–35 minutes at 375".

5. While cake is baking, combine ½ cup sugar, 2 tbsp. water, and rum and bring to a boil.

6. Remove babka from mold when ready, brush on rum glaze, place on cooling rack.

JUST BEFORE SERVING:

Slice and serve. This cake can also be flamed with more rum in the dining room, but in advance, make sure your rum is strong enough to light easily by testing a small quantity in a spoon with a match in the kitchen.

SERVES 6 GENEROUSLY, MORE IF THIN
SLICES ARE USED.

BLACK BOTTOM PIE

4 tbsp. butter
1⅓ cups graham crackers or
vanilla wafers, finely crushed
6 ozs. semi-sweet chocolate,
preferably Swiss
2 tbsp. strong coffee
3 egg yolks
¾ cup granulated sugar

¾ cup milk
1 envelope unflavored gelatin
¼ tsp. salt
3 egg whites
2 tbsp. brandy (optional)
2 tbsp. rum
1 cup heavy cream, whipped

NIGHT BEFORE:

1. Melt butter. Add to finely crushed graham crackers or vanilla wafers, stirring until evenly mixed.
2. Pat on bottom and sides of 9″ pie pan. Make sure crust is evenly spread.
3. Melt 4 ozs. chocolate in saucepan. (Refrigerate remaining chocolate.) Add coffee to melted chocolate and stir.
4. Pour carefully over crust.
5. Beat egg yolks slightly. Cook yolks, ½ cup sugar, and milk in top of double boiler, over boiling water, until mixture is thick enough to coat spoon. Remove from heat.
6. Pour gelatin into ¼ cup cold water. Melt over hot water and add to filling. Cool until mixture starts to set.
7. Add salt to egg whites and beat stiffly. Fold egg whites and brandy (if desired) into filling mixture. Pour filling into chocolate crust.
8. Refrigerate overnight, covered with plastic wrap.

JUST BEFORE SERVING:

1. Fold 2 tbsp. sugar and the rum into whipped cream.
2. Take butter curler or peeler, or whatever implement is easiest for you to sliver chocolate with, and make slivers from remaining chocolate.
3. Spread whipped cream topping over pie. Decorate with chocolate slivers. Serve.

SERVES 8.

BRAZIL NUT WINE CAKE

½ cup butter
2 cups sugar
6 egg yolks, beaten
2 cups sifted flour
½ tsp. baking powder
¼ tsp. salt
1 tsp. powdered cocoa

½ tsp. cinnamon
1 cup milk
¼ cup port wine
1 cup finely chopped Brazil nuts
3 egg whites, beaten

NIGHT BEFORE:

1. With electric mixer, beat butter and sugar until creamy. Add yolks and beat well.
2. Sift flour, baking powder, salt, cocoa, and cinnamon together. Add to first mixture alternately with milk and wine and stir in chopped nuts.
3. Fold in beaten egg whites, gently.
4. Refrigerate overnight, covered.

JUST BEFORE SERVING:

1. Pour batter into greased and floured 10″ cake pan and bake 1 hour at 375°.
2. Serve warm.

SERVES 6−8.

CHEESE PIE

20 vanilla wafers
½ stick (⅛ lb.) butter
1 8-oz. pkg. cream cheese (softened to room temperature)
2½ cups granulated sugar (to taste)

3 tsp. lemon juice
¾ tsp. vanilla
2 eggs, separated
1 pt. sour cream

NIGHT BEFORE:

1. Roll wafers with rolling pin, using back and forth motion, until very fine.

2. Melt butter. Put crumbs into butter and mix well with hands and wooden spoon.
3. Pour mixture into 8″ pie plate and spread thin layer over bottom and sides. Refrigerate.
4. Beat cheese and 2 scoopfuls sugar in electric mixer, slowly adding 1 tsp. lemon juice, vanilla, and egg yolks.
5. Beat egg whites until stiff with hand beater. Add 1 tsp. of lemon.
6. Gradually add beaten whites to mixture, blending carefully.
7. Pour into pan. Bake in 350° oven 20–25 minutes. At end of baking, pie should be white in color.
8. While pie is baking, add 1 tsp. lemon juice and ½ cup of sugar to sour cream and mix well with wooden spoon.
9. Remove pie from oven. Leave oven on. Let pie cool 5 minutes. Then pour sour cream over top.
10. Put pie back into oven 10 minutes.
11. Refrigerate overnight.

JUST BEFORE SERVING:
Let pie sit out for 5–10 minutes, then serve.

SERVES 8 – 12.

COFFEE CAKE WITH ALMOND FROSTING

⋙ *CAKE*

1½ cups all-purpose flour
1 cup granulated sugar
2 tsp. baking powder
½ tsp. salt

1 cup heavy cream
2 eggs
1 tsp. almond extract
1 tsp. vanilla extract

⋙ *FROSTING*

⅓ cup butter
⅔ cup brown sugar, firmly packed

½ cup whole unblanched almonds
3 tbsp. milk
1½ cups sifted powdered sugar

NIGHT BEFORE:

TO MAKE CAKE:

1. Sift flour, measure it, and sift again with granulated sugar, baking powder, and salt.
2. In mixing bowl, whip cream until stiff. Beat in eggs, almond extract, and vanilla.
3. Add sifted dry ingredients to cream mixture and beat in electric mixer until thoroughly blended.
4. Pour batter into a greased 9" round cake pan.
5. Bake in 350° oven 45 minutes or until cake begins to pull away from edge of pan. Insert toothpick into center of cake and make sure that it comes out clean.
6. Let cake stand 10 minutes. Then turn out on wire rack and cool.
7. Store in airtight cake tin or bread box overnight.

NEXT DAY:

TO MAKE FROSTING:

1. Melt butter in saucepan and stir in brown sugar and almonds.
2. Slowly bring mixture to boil and cook 2 minutes over low flame, stirring constantly.
3. Add milk and continue to cook, stirring continuously, until mixture comes to a boil.
4. Remove from heat and cool until lukewarm.
5. Gradually add powdered sugar while beating in mixer. Continue beating until frosting is of a good spreading consistency.
6. Spread over top of cake. Allow icing to drip down sides.

NOTE: Icing can also be made the night before and put on cake. That way, entire cake is a night-before endeavor.

SERVES 10.

CSOKOLADE TORTA
Grated Chocolate Torte

9 *egg whites*
1½ *cups powdered sugar*
½ *cup graham cracker crumbs*
½ *cup grated chocolate (bitter-sweet is suggested, but any chocolate will do, according to your preference)*

2 *tbsp. flour*
1 *tsp. baking powder*
½ *lb. ground nuts*
¼ *cup red wine*
Juice of 1 lemon
Butter

NIGHT BEFORE:

1. In large bowl of electric mixer, beat egg whites until stiff.
2. Add sugar and beat.
3. In separate bowl mix together cracker crumbs, grated chocolate, flour, baking powder, and nuts.
4. Fold dry ingredients gently into egg whites. Add wine and lemon juice. Mix gently.
5. Pour into 2 9″ cake pans lined with waxed paper and greased with butter.
6. Bake at 350° 40 minutes. Cool.
7. Put torte on rimmed pan or tray. Spread icing between layers. Pour icing over torte and refrigerate.
8. When icing has solidified enough, spread up sides.
9. Refrigerate until ready to serve.

JUST BEFORE SERVING:

Remove torte to serving platter and serve.

Suggested Icings
Chocolate Cream Cheese Icing (*below*)
Mocha Frosting from Pecan Torte Wanda (page 160)
Almond Frosting from Coffee Cake (page 152)
S E R V E S   6 – 8 .

⌐§ CHOCOLATE CREAM CHEESE ICING

3 ozs. semisweet chocolate
3 ozs. cream cheese (1 small pkg.), softened at room temperature

¼ cup milk
4 cups powdered sugar
½ tsp. salt

1. Melt chocolate in double boiler over hot water.
2. In bowl, pour milk into softened cream cheese. Mix well, gradually adding powdered sugar and salt, stirring until creamy.
3. Pour melted chocolate into cream cheese mixture and beat until smooth and ready to be spread.
4. Spread when cake is slightly warm.

MAKES APPROXIMATELY 2 CUPS.

ITALIAN RICOTTA CHEESE CAKE

1½ lbs. Ricotta cheese
1¼ cups finest granulated sugar
¼ cup Kahlua

¼ cup chopped candied fruits
¼ cup blanched almonds
12 ladyfingers

NIGHT BEFORE:

1. With electric mixer beat cheese, sugar, and Kahlua until smooth.
2. Add candied fruits and almonds.
3. Butter round 1½-qt. mold, and line bottom and sides with split ladyfingers.
4. Pour in cheese mixture, and then cover top with remaining ladyfingers.
5. Refrigerate overnight, covered with sheet of waxed paper.

JUST BEFORE SERVING:

Turn out onto serving platter.

MAKES ENOUGH FOR A ROUND
1½ - QT. MOLD.

LINZER TÉSZTA
Linzer Meringue Cake

This recipe requires an 11" by 15" by 1" jelly roll pan.

3 *cups flour (sifted measure)*	5 *eggs, separated*
1 *tsp. baking powder*	1 *tsp. vanilla extract*
1 *cup plus 2 tbsp. sugar*	6 *tbsp. sour cream*
¼ *lb. butter*	1½ *cups raspberry preserves*
¼ *lb. vegetable shortening*	½ *cup ground walnuts*

NIGHT BEFORE:

1. Sift together into mixing bowl flour, baking powder, and 2 tbsp. sugar.
2. Cut butter and shortening into dry ingredients.
3. Separately, mix together egg yolks, vanilla extract, and sour cream.
4. Now mix yolk mixture into dry ingredients, knead together, then refrigerate, in mixing bowl, 1 hour.
5. Preheat oven to 350° while dough is chilling. Butter bottom and sides of pan.
6. Roll dough out on floured board to approximate size of pan. Reverse into pan and smooth out to an even thickness by hand.
7. Spread entire top of dough evenly with raspberry preserves. Bake in preheated oven for 30 minutes.
8. Remove cake from oven, and leaving in jelly roll pan, cover with sheet of waxed paper and store at room temperature overnight.

JUST BEFORE SERVING:

1. Beat egg whites, adding 1 cup sugar gradually until stiff peaks are formed.
2. Preheat oven to 350°.
3. Spread egg white mixture evenly over top of preserves, then sprinkle with ground walnuts.
4. Bake 15 minutes or until egg whites turn pale brown.
5. Cut portions and serve directly from pan.

S E R V E S   6 – 8 .

MANDARIN ORANGE CHIFFON PIE

◄§ *9″ PIE SHELL*

1½ *cups all-purpose flour, sifted*
½ *tsp. salt*
½ *cup vegetable shortening*

3 *tbsp. orange juice (fresh if possible, completely strained)*

◄§ *FILLING*

2 *11-oz. cans mandarin oranges, drained, and their syrup (you will have some fruit left over)*
1 *envelope unflavored gelatin*
4 *eggs, separated*
¾ *cup granulated sugar*

⅛ *tsp. salt*
1 *tbsp. lemon juice*
½ *cup heavy cream*
2 *tsp. Cointreau (optional)*
½ *cup flaked coconut, toasted*

NIGHT BEFORE:

TO MAKE PIE SHELL:

1. Preheat oven to 425°.
2. Add salt to already sifted flour and resift into large mixing bowl.
3. With pastry blender or with 2 knives, work in shortening until mixture is consistency of tiny peas.
4. Sprinkle orange juice in, 1 tbsp. at a time, tossing mixture lightly and stirring with fork. Add juice each time to driest part of mixture. Dough should be just moist enough to hold together when pressed gently with a fork.
5. With your hands shape dough into smooth ball.
6. Roll dough between 2 sheets of foil or waxed paper. Roll lightly from center out in all directions to ⅛″ thickness, making an 11″ circle. Fold rolled dough in half and ease it gently into pie pan, with fold in center. Unfold dough and carefully press out air pockets with your fingertips. Trim excess dough from edge, then crimp as desired. Refrigerate until ready to fill.

TO MAKE FILLING:

1. Pour syrup of 1 can mandarins into measuring cup. Add enough cold water to reach 1-cup measurement.
2. Pour gelatin into ¼ cup cold water.

3. In top of double boiler, beat egg yolks with rotary beater until light and fluffy.

4. Stir in sugar, salt, syrup mixture, and lemon juice.

5. Cook over hot water until mixture thickens, stirring constantly.

6. Add gelatin, which has softened. Cook and stir until gelatin dissolves. Cool in refrigerator.

7. Put mandarins from 1 can into plastic container. Cover and refrigerate overnight.

8. Cut mandarins from second can into small pieces.

9. Take mixture from refrigerator and gently fold mandarin pieces into this custard.

10. In electric mixer, beat egg whites until they form soft peaks.

11. Fold egg whites into fruit-custard.

12. Pour into cool pie shell. Refrigerate overnight.

JUST BEFORE SERVING:

1. Whip heavy cream, adding Cointreau or any orange-flavored liqueur if desired.

2. Garnish pie with whipped cream and mandarins. Sprinkle with toasted cocoanut.

3. Serve immediately.

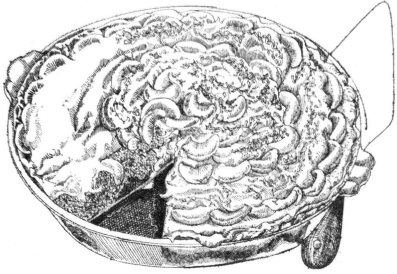

PECAN TORTE WANDA

14 *large eggs, separated*   *6 full cups pecans*
3 *heaping cups granulated sugar*   ¼ *cup flour*

NIGHT BEFORE:
1. Grease 3 9″ cake pans heavily (pans should have loosening blade).
2. In large bowl, beat egg yolks into sugar until mixture is thick and lemon-colored.
3. Add flour, beating constantly.
4. Beat egg whites until stiff.
5. Grate pecans. Stir grated nuts ⅓ at a time into sugar mixture, alternating with egg whites.
6. Pour into pans and bake in 350° oven 20 minutes. Then push in sides slightly, all around pans, with back of spoon.
7. Bake another 20–25 minutes until cakes spring back when lightly touched with finger.
8. Let cakes sit out to cool completely.
9. Spread filling between torte layers.
10. Put torte on rimmed pan or tray. *Pour* icing over torte. (Be sure enough icing runs down sides to pick up after it cools).
11. Refrigerate until icing solidifies enough to spread up sides.
12. Keep torte in refrigerator until ready to serve.

JUST BEFORE SERVING:
Remove torte to serving platter and serve.

SERVES 12.

⋖ *TORTE VARIATION*
For this you need a jelly roll pan.
2½ *cups pecans*   1¼ *cups granulated sugar*
6 *eggs, separated*

1. Grease pan.
2. Beat egg yolks into sugar, following procedure for Pecan Torte Wanda.

3. Grate pecans. Add to mixture, alternating with stiffly beaten egg whites.
4. Bake in 350° oven 45 minutes.
5. Cool. Add icing, if desired. Refrigerate overnight.
6. Serve with whipped cream if not frosted.

⇜ *MOCHA FILLING AND FROSTING*

1 lb. unsalted butter, softened   *9 egg yolks*
  several hours or overnight   *2 cups strong coffee*
1½" vanilla bean, split and put *2 cups powdered sugar*
  into softening butter

1. In electric mixer, mix softened butter—including vanilla bean— with egg yolks added 1 at a time.
2. Bring coffee to a boil, then simmer.
3. To butter and egg mixture, add alternately 1 tbsp. coffee with 1 tbsp. sugar, beating thoroughly all the while.
4. Remove vanilla bean from mixture.
5. Spread frosting between torte layers, and over sides and top, as indicated in basic torte recipe.

⇜ *CHOCOLATE FILLING*

½ lb. unsalted butter, softened *6 tbsp. powdered sugar, sifted*
¼ cup cocoa, sifted

Stir until glossy. Set aside and do not chill.

⇜ *CHOCOLATE ICING*

10 ozs. semi-sweet chocolate   *1 cup powdered sugar*
1 pt. light cream

1. Melt ingredients over very low fire.
2. When mixture comes to boil, stir constantly and cook 10 minutes.
3. Set aside to cool.

RAISIN BANANA CAKE LOAF
With Rum

¼ lb. butter
1⅔ cups granulated sugar
2 eggs
¼ tsp. salt
½ tsp. baking soda
1½ tsp. baking powder
4 tbsp. sour cream
1 cup blended or mashed
  banana pulp

2 cups cake flour (sifted
  measure)
1 tsp. almond extract
2 cups raisins
2 tbsp. dark rum
1 tbsp. powdered confectioners
  sugar

NIGHT BEFORE:

1. Cream butter and sugar together with electric mixer.
2. Beat eggs lightly in separate bowl with whisk, then add to mixture.
3. Add salt. Mix thoroughly.
4. Combine baking soda, baking powder, and sour cream in separate bowl. Mix thoroughly until powders dissolve. Stir into main mixture.
5. With mixer running at medium speed, add banana pulp, then sifted flour, a little at a time. Now add almond extract, raisins, and rum.
6. Preheat oven to 350°.
7. Pour mixture into buttered loaf pan, 9½" by 5½" by 2½", and bake 1½ hours. Remove from oven, remove cake from pan, and cool on rack.
8. When cool, wrap tightly in plastic wrap and refrigerate overnight.

JUST BEFORE SERVING:

1. Remove cake from refrigerator and allow to return to room temperature, unwrapped.
2. Dust top with powdered sugar and serve.

RAISIN-EGG BREAD LOAF

4 packages dry yeast (or 2 ozs.   1 pinch saffron
   fresh yeast)   5 cups flour
1 cup warm milk   ¼ lb. butter (softened)
¾ cup sugar   ½ cup melted butter
1 tsp. salt   2 cups white raisins
1 tsp. vanilla extract   1 egg yolk
1 tsp. grated lemon rind   1 tbsp. light cream
3 eggs   ½ cup blanched almonds

NIGHT BEFORE:

1. Dissolve dry yeast in warm (not boiling hot) milk in bottom
   of large mixing bowl. Then blend in ½ cup sugar, the salt,
   vanilla extract, and lemond rind. Beat in eggs and saffron
   (crushed in 1 tbsp. warm water).

   If using fresh yeast, cream it with salt and ½ cup of sugar
   until a thick syrup is formed. Then add milk and the vanilla,
   lemon rind, eggs, and crushed saffron.

2. Add flour, mixing thoroughly with liquid until dough is formed,
   then work in softened butter. Knead dough 10–12 minutes
   until it is shiny and elastic, and comes away from sides of bowl
   cleanly.

3. Cover bowl with a towel and place in warm, draft-free place
   to rise. This should take about 45 minutes–1 hour—dough
   must double in bulk before you proceed.

4. Preheat oven to 350°. Butter 2 9″ by 5″ by 3″ loaf pans.

5. Dust table or counter surface with flour. Roll out dough into
   large square, ¼″ thick. Brush surface with melted butter.
   Spread raisins evenly over surface. Roll up dough like jelly roll.

6. Press roll of dough down with rolling pin to thickness of 1″.
   Cut lengthwise into 3 long strips. Then cut each strip in half to
   make total of 6 strips. Braid 3 of the strips together (starting
   from middle) for each loaf. Fit each braided loaf into pan and
   allow to rise until double in bulk.

7. Beat egg yolk with cream. Brush tops of risen loaves with

mixture. Scatter almonds over top, then sprinkle remaining ¼ cup of sugar over loaves.

8. Now bake in middle level of preheated oven about 45 minutes. Tops should be deep golden brown, and almonds should look toasted.

9. When loaves are baked, remove from pans immediately and place on cooling racks. Loaves may be wrapped and frozen, or simply kept in airtight container if they are to be used within a day or two.

JUST BEFORE SERVING:

1. *As bread:* Heat in 350° oven 10 minutes, slice and serve.

2. *As dessert:* Slice, top each slice with scoop of vanilla ice cream, pour 1 tbsp. hot brandy over each scoop, and serve.

MAKES 2 9″-BY-5″-BY-3″ LOAVES.

SPRINGERLE COOKIES

You must begin these *two* nights before, unless you are willing to take your chances with chilling the dough in your freezer for a few hours to substitute for an overnight in the refrigerator. You will require either a wooden rolling pin with inset springerle cookie designs, or some individual wooden springerle molding boards. Perhaps you have some hanging on your kitchen wall as decorations.

2½ cups sifted white all-purpose   *1½ cups granulated sugar*
   flour   *1 tsp. grated orange rind*
¾ tsp. baking powder   *½ tsp. grated lemon rind*
½ tsp. salt   *2 tbsp. anise seeds*
3 eggs

TWO NIGHTS BEFORE:

1. Sift flour, baking powder, and salt together into a bowl.

2. With electric beater, beat together the eggs, sugar, orange and lemon rind about 20 minutes at medium speed. Then, without turning off beaters, add dry ingredients a little at a time until dough is formed.

3. Roll dough into ball, flour outside, and wrap in waxed paper.
4. Refrigerate overnight.

NIGHT BEFORE:

1. Put springerle molds or rolling pin into freezing compartment.
2. Flour pastry board or cloth.
3. Roll out ball of dough to ½″ thickness with plain rolling pin, keeping it in as close to a rectangular shape as possible.
4. Sprinkle molds or springerle rolling pin with flour. Press firmly into surface of dough to make designs in relief.
5. Cut cookies apart from each other with dough separator or knife.
6. Butter cookie sheets, and sprinkle anise seeds over them evenly.
7. Place cookies on sheets, without sides touching, and let stand overnight at room temperature.

JUST BEFORE SERVING:

1. Preheat oven to 325°.
2. Bake cookies 15 minutes and serve warm.

MAKES ABOUT 2 DOZEN COOKIES.

SWISS APPLE ROLL

⋖§ DOUGH

2 tbsp. butter	2 eggs, beaten
½ cup milk	1 package dry yeast
¼ cup sugar	3 cups all-purpose flour
1 tsp. salt	

⋖§ FILLING

½ lb. dried apples	¼ tsp. cinnamon
¼ lb. dried apricots	½ tsp. nutmeg
¼ cup raisins	¼ cup sugar
½ cup dried figs	2 tbsp. cognac
¼ cup chopped walnuts	½ cup white wine
2 tbsp. lemon juice	

NIGHT BEFORE:

TO MAKE DOUGH:

1. Stir butter in milk in saucepan over medium-low flame until butter melts. Stir in sugar, salt, and 1 beaten egg, all off heat. Allow to cool.
2. While milk mixture is cooling, dissolve yeast powder in 4 tbsp. warm (not hot) water. Then stir it into cooled milk mixture.
3. Beat in flour a little at a time to make soft dough.
4. Knead dough on a floured board, then put into large mixing bowl, cover with cloth, and allow to rise in a warm, draft-free place until doubled in bulk.

TO MAKE FILLING:

1. Simmer apples and apricots in water until tender. Drain.
2. Run apples, apricots, raisins, and figs through coarsest blade of meat grinder.
3. Blend in walnuts, lemon juice, cinnamon, nutmeg, sugar, and cognac. Finally add wine to make a thick paste.

TO MAKE ROLL:

1. Roll dough out on floured board into 12" square. Spread square of dough with filling.
2. Fold in ends and roll up. Prick top of roll with fork at 1" intervals. Brush top with remaining beaten egg. Allow to rise again until bulk doubles.
3. While roll dough is rising, preheat oven to 350°.
4. Place roll on buttered cookie sheet or jelly roll pan. Bake 30 minutes until brown. Cool on rack.

JUST BEFORE SERVING:

Sprinkle top with a half-and-half mixture of cinnamon and granulated sugar, if desired. Slice and serve.

MAKES 1 12" ROLL — SERVES 6.

XI

OTHER DESSERTS

XI

ALMOND BLANCMANGE
With Peaches

4½-oz. can blanched almonds
2 envelopes unflavored gelatin
1 cup heavy cream
½ cup granulated sugar

3 tsp. almond extract
1 tsp. vanilla extract
6 tbsp. Cointreau
4 cups sliced peaches

NIGHT BEFORE:

1. Soak almonds in 1½ cups cold water 1 hour.
2. Put almonds and water in blender and blend 1 minute at low speed.
3. Change to high speed for 2–3 minutes until mixture is creamy.
4. Pour gelatin into ¼ cup cold water.
5. Place gelatin into top of double boiler over boiling water. Add heavy cream and sugar, stirring constantly.
6. When gelatin is melted, remove from fire and mix in almond mixture, almond extract, vanilla extract, and 2 tbsp. Cointreau. Stir until smooth.
7. Pour into individual molds or oiled 3-cup ring mold. If using individual molds, fill only ¾ full (dessert is rich).
8. Refrigerate overnight.
9. Soak peaches in 4 tbsp. Cointreau in covered container overnight.

JUST BEFORE SERVING:

1. Unmold by either running knife around edge of molds or setting them briefly in hot water.
2. If using individual molds, place blancmange on plates, surround

with peaches, and pour Cointreau marinade lightly over. If using ring mold, unmold and fill center with peaches.

SERVES 6.

APPLE SAUCE

12 *medium apples*
¾ *cup apricot preserves*
1 *tbsp. vanilla extract*
1 *tbsp. lemon juice*

½ *cup sugar*
2 *tbsp. butter*
1 *tsp. cinnamon*

NIGHT BEFORE:

1. Peel, core, and quarter apples, then slice each quarter into 3 or 4 pieces.
2. Cook apples over low heat in heavy enameled saucepan, covered, about 20 minutes, stirring occasionally.
3. While apples are cooking, force apricot preserves through sieve into measuring cup to produce ½ cup of glaze.
4. After the 20 minutes cooking time, raise heat to high, allow apple sauce to simmer while stirring in thoroughly the apricot glaze, vanilla, lemon juice, sugar, butter, and cinnamon.
5. Remove from heat and refrigerate in covered container.

JUST BEFORE SERVING:

This apple sauce can be used as a pie filling, a cold dessert (top with large spoonful of sour cream and sprinkle with brown sugar), or hot with roast pork, duck, or other meats.

MAKES APPROX. 2 QTS.

APRICOT MOUSSE

1 *lb. dried apricots*
¾ *cup granulated sugar*
3 *egg whites*
¼ *cup slivered almonds*

4 *ozs. apricot brandy (optional)*
6 *fresh or canned apricot*
   halves

NIGHT BEFORE:

1. Simmer apricots in 2 qts. water uncovered 40 minutes.
2. Add sugar and simmer 10 more minutes.
3. Pour off water and allow apricots to cool. Then transfer to blender jar.
4. Blend in electric blender to make a purée. Refrigerate purée overnight.

JUST BEFORE SERVING:

1. Beat egg whites until they form soft peaks.
2. Mix almonds into purée, then fold purée into egg whites thoroughly. Add apricot brandy if desired.
3. Spoon the mousse into individual sherbet glasses, and top each with an apricot half. This may be done a little in advance and refrigerated during dinner, but once the whites are folded in, the mousse should not sit any longer than a couple of hours.

SERVES 6.

BOMBE ROTHSCHILD

This dessert tastes delicious, but its primary value is the stupendous effect it creates when presented. You need a tall, 2-qt. mold—preferably a conical one—*not* hollow at the center. Served up covered with snowy white meringues, traced with driblets of brown-and-gold sugar syrup, this bombe is a veritable Mont Blanc of the dinner table. Then when opened, it reveals the rich surprise of the concealed chocolate shavings in the core. The recipe is quite easy to make; when your guests ask you how you did it, just be mysterious.

2 qts. best-quality French vanilla ice cream
1 14-oz. solid bar (or equivalent in smaller sizes, but largest bar is much easier to work with)

Swiss semisweet or bittersweet chocolate, kept at room temperature
2 cups granulated sugar

NIGHT BEFORE:

1. Place ice cream into mold, packing down as tightly as possible.
2. Freeze at least 2 hours.

3. Meanwhile, angle chocolate bar (it is 6"–8" long) into a shallow wooden bowl. With a French butter curler or sharp knife, make shavings by drawing curler or knife along surface of chocolate bar from top to bottom with firm pressure. When shavings in bottom of bowl are ½" deep, transfer to another bowl and refrigerate. Continue shaving and refrigerating the shavings until you have 2 cups of loose shavings. (This should use up about half the chocolate bar.)

4. Take mold from freezer. Dig a hole about 1" in diameter down the center of the ice cream, not quite to the bottom. Best implement for this is a long-handled iced tea spoon, frequently dipped in hot water.

5. Fill hole with shavings by sliding through waxed-paper funnel. Leave ¼" at top and fill this with ice cream.

6. Freeze overnight.

7. Make meringues. Make chocolate sauce if you prefer to do it now.

JUST BEFORE SERVING:

1. Unmold ice cream by dipping mold in hot water 1 minute.

2. Cover with meringues (see below).

3. Melt sugar in saucepan until it reaches 290° on candy thermometer.

4. Dribble hot sugar syrup over meringues, paying special attention to cracks between. This makes meringues adhere to each other, thus forming a beautiful meringue shell over entire dessert.

5. Keep bombe in freezer until ready to serve. It will melt if merely refrigerated.

6. Serve with hot Sauce Au Chocolat Elégante. We recommend bringing bombe to table, cutting it open so guests can see chocolate shavings pour out, and serving in slices. Sauce can be served in sauce server or small pitcher.

SERVES 10–12.

◄ SAUCE AU CHOCOLAT ELÉGANTE

Remainder of chocolate bar after   6 drops vanilla extract
  shavings are made   ½ cup granulated sugar
½ cup very strong coffee

1. In double boiler melt chocolate into coffee. Add vanilla extract and sugar (to taste).
2. Stir with wooden spoon until smooth.

NOTE: Sauce may be prepared the night before and reheated before serving.

MAKES ABOUT 2 CUPS SAUCE.

◄ MERINGUES

8 egg whites   Shortening
1 lb. confectioners powdered   Flour
  sugar

1. Beat egg whites until they form soft peaks.
2. Sprinkle on sugar while continuing to beat, until all sugar is absorbed in mixture.
3. Spoon out onto greased and lightly floured cookie sheet.
4. Bake in 200° oven 2 hours.
5. Remove from oven. Store in airtight container until used.

NOTE: For best results, bake meringues overnight in oven with only pilot light heat.

MAKES ABOUT 20—24 MERINGUES,
DEPENDING ON SIZE.

BRITISH HARD SAUCE

This very sweet sauce is ideal as a garnish for hot desserts such as hot apple pie, cobbler, etc.

¼ lb. butter   ½ tsp. vanilla extract
2 cups confectioners powdered   ¼ tsp. ground nutmeg
  sugar   ¼ cup cognac
⅛ tsp. salt   ½ cup heavy cream

NIGHT BEFORE:

1. Soften butter, then beat with electric mixer until creamy.
2. Sift sugar slowly into butter, beating all the while.
3. Beat in salt, vanilla, nutmeg, and cognac.
4. Finally beat in cream, and beat until very smooth.
5. Transfer to decorative serving bowl and refrigerate overnight, covered with waxed paper.

JUST BEFORE SERVING:
Serve directly from chilled bowl.

MAKES 2 CUPS.

CANTON FRUIT CUP

2 8-oz. cans pineapple chunks
4 navel oranges, peeled and
   skinned, cut up

4 bananas, peeled and sliced
2 pieces preserved ginger candy,
   minced

NIGHT BEFORE:

1. Mix all ingredients.
2. Refrigerate overnight in covered container.

JUST BEFORE SERVING:

1. Divide into sherbet cups.
2. Serve with gaily decorated toothpicks.

SERVES 6.

CRANBERRY KISSEL
Classic Russian Dessert

4 cups fresh cranberries, washed
1½ cups granulated sugar
½ cup raspberry syrup

2 tbsp. cornstarch
½ pt. heavy cream

NIGHT BEFORE:

1. Cover fruit in saucepan with cold water.
2. Bring to boil, then reduce heat and simmer exactly 10 minutes.
3. Rub cooked cranberries through medium-fine sieve.

4. Add sugar and raspberry syrup, bring purée to boil, then turn off heat.
5. Mix cornstarch with a little water into smooth paste. Mix it into the purée and simmer 4 minutes, stirring constantly. Pour into individual serving cups and refrigerate overnight.

JUST BEFORE SERVING:

1. Whip heavy cream until soft peaks are formed.
2. Put generous spoonful of cream on surface of each cup of kissel.
3. Serve cold.

S E R V E S   6 .

CRÈME BRÛLÉE

6 *egg yolks*	½ *tsp. almond extract*
1 *cup granulated sugar*	1½ *cups brown sugar*
2 *cups heavy cream*	1 *tbsp. powdered cinnamon*

NIGHT BEFORE:

1. Preheat oven to 275°.
2. Beat egg yolks and granulated sugar with electric mixer until pale yellow and rather thick.
3. Heat cream separately up to boiling point.
4. Slowly add hot cream to egg yolk mixture while continuing to beat. Add almond extract.
5. Pour mixture into saucepan, and stir over medium heat until custard thickens. Remove from heat and pour into shallow oven proof dish (the rectangular kind is best).
6. Bake at 275° about 1 hour, or until custard sets. A cake needle plunged into custard should come out clean.
7. When custard is set, remove from oven and refrigerate overnight.

JUST BEFORE SERVING:

1. Prepare brown sugar by breaking up all lumps and tossing in mixing bowl with fork to loosen. Toss in and mix cinnamon with sugar.

2. Just before dessert is to be served, spread sugar-cinnamon in layer across top of cold custard.
3. Hold under broiler (on high) just long enough to melt top of brown sugar. Then serve immediately.

NOTE: You can do the brown sugar operation the night before too, and serve the whole thing cold, but in that case you must let the custard cool before adding and toasting the sugar.

S E R V E S 6 .

CRÈME DE ABACATE
Avocado Cream Dessert

3 *ripe avocados*
6 *tbsp. sugar*
1 *tsp. vanilla*

Juice of 1 lemon
6 *tbsp. crushed almonds*

NIGHT BEFORE:

1. Peel avocados, remove seeds, and put in blender with sugar, vanilla, and lemon juice.
2. Put into glass bowl or in individual sherbet cups.
3. Chill overnight in refrigerator.

JUST BEFORE SERVING:

Garnish with crushed almonds and serve cold.

S E R V E S 6 .

CRÈME RENVERSÉE AU CARAMEL
Caramel Custard with Raisins

¾ *cup granulated sugar*
2 *eggs*
3 *egg yolks*
⅛ *tsp. salt*

1 *tsp. vanilla extract (or 2*
vanilla beans, split and
scraped out)
1½ *cups milk*
1 *cup white raisins*

NIGHT BEFORE:

1. Melt sugar over medium heat until it browns. Slowly stir in ¾ cup boiling water, a little at a time. Simmer mixture 3 or 4

minutes, then pour into 1-qt. baking dish. Pick up baking dish with pot holders and tilt it all around to coat sides with caramel.

2. In mixing bowl beat eggs, egg yolks, salt, and vanilla thoroughly. Now heat milk (do not boil), and pour slowly into egg mixture, beating all the while. If you use an electric mixer this is easy; otherwise you have to add a little milk, then pick up the beater, beat it in, and keep repeating the process.

3. When all the milk is blended, turn off beater, stir in raisins.

4. Preheat oven to 250°. Pour custard into baking dish, or individual custard cups, in which case divide ingredients equally among cups, being careful that not too many raisins wind up in one cup, leaving another barren of them!

5. Place dish in shallow pan of water, and bake 1 hour. Custard is ready when knife or needle comes out clean. Refrigerate overnight.

JUST BEFORE SERVING:

Reverse onto serving platter and serve. You may have to loosen by running a knife around the inside edges first.

S E R V E S   6 .

COEURS À LA CRÈME

This dish looks especially charming made and served in heart-shaped wicker basket molds, but any individual molds can be used. You will need 12 1-ft.-long pieces of cheesecloth.

1 8-oz. pkg. cream cheese, soft- ened at room temperature	1 vanilla bean, split, seeds scraped off
2 tbsp. light cream	1 cup heavy cream, whipped
1 cup powdered sugar	2 pkgs. frozen strawberries
⅛ tsp. salt	½ cup kirsch
2 tbsp. lemon juice	

NIGHT BEFORE:

1. Blend cream cheese, light cream, and sugar in electric mixer until soft and smooth.

2. Add salt, lemon juice, and vanilla bean seeds.
3. Add whipped cream, folding thoroughly until mixture is smooth.
4. Put double layer of damp cheesecloth into 6 individual molds.
5. Pour mixture into molds. If using wicker baskets, place baskets on plate for draining purposes. If using regular molds, make sure they have been rinsed in very cold or ice water before mixture is poured in. Fold cheesecloth so mixture and molds are fully wrapped.
6. Refrigerate overnight. (Keep baskets on raised rack over receptacle to catch drainage.)

JUST BEFORE SERVING:
1. Defrost berries and add all liqueur to its juice. Pour into sauce server.
2. Bring baskets to table. Undo cheesecloth. Flip baskets over and unmold onto plates. Serve with sauce. (If regular molds are used, unmold in kitchen.)

SERVES 6.

FROZEN BAVARIAN CREAM WITH CRANBERRY-ORANGE SAUCE

4 egg whites
1 cup granulated sugar
⅛ tsp. salt
2 cups heavy cream

2 tsp. vanilla extract
1 tsp. almond extract
2 tsp. Grand Marnier or Cointreau

NIGHT BEFORE:
1. Refrigerate ring mold.
2. Separate eggs. Place egg whites in small bowl of electric mixer and let sit at room temperature 1 hour.
3. Combine sugar and ⅓ cup water in saucepan, and cook over low heat, stirring continually, until sugar is dissolved.
4. Bring to boil over medium heat. Add candy thermometer. Boil, uncovered, until thermometer registers 236°. Do not stir.
5. Meanwhile, beat egg whites and salt at high speed until stiff peaks are formed.

6. Pour sugar syrup gradually over egg whites, beating constantly until mixture forms very stiff peaks.
7. Refrigerate, covered, 30 minutes.
8. In medium-sized bowl, beat cream with vanilla and almond extracts and Grand Marnier until stiff.
9. With wire whisk or rubber scraper, gently fold whipped cream into egg-white mixture until thoroughly combined.
10. Turn into chilled ring mold.
11. Cover with foil and freeze overnight.

JUST BEFORE SERVING:

1. Unmold by running a small spatula around edges of mold.
2. Invert on serving platter and freeze until serving time.
3. Serve with hot Cranberry-Orange Sauce.

SERVES 6.

⋅§ CRANBERRY-ORANGE SAUCE

2 cups fresh cranberries (raspberries, blackberries, sliced
strawberries, or blueberries may
be substituted)
1 cup granulated sugar

1 tbsp. orange peel, grated
½ cup walnuts, chopped
3 tbsp. light corn syrup
2 tbsp. Grand Marnier or
Cointreau

NIGHT BEFORE:

1. Wash berries. Remove stems. Drain.
2. Combine sugar and 1 cup water in saucepan. Cook over low heat, stirring continually, until sugar is dissolved.
3. Bring to boil over medium heat. Boil, uncovered, 10 minutes or until syrup thickens slightly. Do not stir.
4. Add berries, orange peel, and walnuts to sugar syrup. Cook gently 5 minutes, until berries begin to burst.
5. Remove from heat. Stir in corn syrup and Grand Marnier.
6. Refrigerate overnight in covered container.

JUST BEFORE SERVING:

Heat sauce over very low flame. Keep warm until serving time.

MAKES ABOUT 2 ½ CUPS.

GOOSEBERRY WHIP

1 qt. ripe green gooseberries	2 cups heavy cream
¾ cup brown sugar	1 tsp. almond extract

NIGHT BEFORE:
1. Wash berries thoroughly. Snip off tops and tails with scissors.
2. In top of double boiler, place berries, sugar, and 1 cup water and cook over boiling water 15 minutes or until tender.
3. Mash through fine sieve with wooden spoon.
4. Refrigerate overnight in covered container.

JUST BEFORE SERVING:
1. Beat cream until stiff and fold into gooseberry mixture.
2. Add almond extract and fold once again.
3. Serve in chilled sherbet dishes immediately.

S E R V E S 6.

INDIAN PUDDING

1 qt. milk	½ tsp. cinnamon
¼ cup corn meal	½ tsp. nutmeg (ground)
⅔ cup maple syrup	¼ cup melted butter
¼ cup sugar	Raspberry syrup
1 tsp. salt	

NIGHT BEFORE:
1. Preheat oven to 250°.
2. Scald 1 pt. milk in top of double boiler directly over flame. Then remove from flame and put over simmering water.
3. Mix corn meal with ½ cup of cold milk, then stir mixture into scalded milk, stirring the whole time. Allow to cook 15 minutes, stirring occasionally.
4. Blend in maple syrup, sugar, salt, cinnamon, nutmeg, and butter.
5. Add remaining cold milk to pudding mixture and pour into buttered 1½-qt. baking dish. Bake standing in pan of hot water 3 hours. Refrigerate overnight.

JUST BEFORE SERVING:
1. Remove from refrigerator and let stand about 30 minutes to reach room temperature.
2. Stand baking dish in pan of hot water over flame; simmer water 10 minutes.
3. Serve with hot raspberry syrup to pour over each portion.

SERVES 6.

MOUSSE AU CHOCOLAT
Chocolate Mousse

¼ cup sugar
4 ozs. sweet chocolate
⅛ tsp. vanilla extract

¼ tsp. nutmeg (ground)
2 egg whites
2 cups heavy cream, chilled

NIGHT BEFORE:
1. Melt sugar in 1 tbsp. water over medium heat until clear (but not brown) syrup is formed.
2. Melt chocolate over simmering water in top of double boiler. Then add syrup to chocolate, blend thoroughly, and remove from heat. Add vanilla. Allow to cool to room temperature.
3. Beat egg whites until they form soft peaks.
4. Fold cooled chocolate mixture into whites gently but thoroughly enough to make sure no lumps of chocolate or pockets of white remain.
5. Whip heavy cream until it forms soft peaks. Fold whipped cream into mousse.
6. Turn mousse into individual sherbet glasses and chill thoroughly overnight.
7. Or, turn mousse into decorative mold and put in freezer overnight. Result is a light frozen ice cream.

JUST BEFORE SERVING:
1. Simply serve mousse in sherbet cups.
2. Or, unmold frozen mousse by dipping mold in hot water and reversing onto serving platter. Cut at the table and serve.

SERVES 6.

POTS DE CRÈME AU CHOCOLAT

This rich chocolate dessert is usually made and served in individual ceramic cups designed specifically for this dish. However, it works perfectly well in individual custard cups.

2 cups heavy cream	*⅓ cup sugar*
4 1-oz. squares semisweet cooking chocolate	*⅛ tsp. salt*
	3 tsp. vanilla extract
6 egg yolks	*½ cup ground toasted almonds*

NIGHT BEFORE:

1. Heat all but ¼ cup cream in saucepan until hot but not boiling. Add chocolate squares and stir until they melt and blend well with cream.
2. In separate bowl, beat egg yolks with electric mixer until light yellow. Continuing beating, add sugar and salt gradually. Then add the reserved ¼ cup cream.

3. Now stir into the bowl the hot chocolate cream and vanilla extract.
4. Preheat oven to 325°.
5. Pour mixture into individual *pots*, set them in baking pan, and pour into pan about 1″ boiling water.
6. Cover *pots* either with their own covers, or with a sheet of foil, and bake about 20 minutes, or until a cake testing needle comes out clean.
7. Remove from oven, uncover, sprinkle top of each *pot* with toasted almonds, and refrigerate overnight covered with waxed paper or plastic wrap. (These will keep several days if necessary.)

JUST BEFORE SERVING:
Serve as is.

SERVES 6.

RAISIN-BREAD PUDDING

1 *cup brown sugar*	¼ *tsp. ground cinnamon*
3 *slices white bread*	3 *eggs*
3 *tbsp. butter*	2 *cups milk*
1 *cup white raisins*	1 *tsp. vanilla extract*
¼ *cup blanched slivered almonds*	*Pinch of salt*
1 *tbsp. grated orange rind*	

NIGHT BEFORE:
1. In top of double boiler over simmering water, place brown sugar evenly across bottom.
2. Butter bread slices, using all the butter, then cut them into ½″ squares and toss over sugar. Now sprinkle on raisins, almonds, orange rind, and cinnamon.
3. Beat together eggs, milk, vanilla, and salt. Pour mixture into first mixture. Do not stir.
4. Cover and cook over simmering water 1 hour.
5. Remove and refrigerate overnight in same pan, covered with plastic wrap.

JUST BEFORE SERVING:

Cold: Simply transfer to serving dish as is and serve.

Hot: Return to double boiler over simmering water and heat through before serving.

S E R V E S   6 .

ROUGE ET BLANC SUPRÊME
Raspberry and Coconut Jelled Dessert

In the simplest terms, this is merely a two-tone Jello! But it requires some close attention to detail and tastes far better than a packaged gelatin dessert mix. When you have made this once, you will quickly see how you can improve on the decorative effects. You can use all kinds of molds, you can make individual servings in small molds, you can prepare it in many layers—rather than only two—for a striped effect. And you can devise a way of setting the gelatin in the mold at an angle to give the layers a bias effect when unmolded. Try!

2 cups fresh raspberries or 2 pkgs. frozen raspberries
½ cup granulated sugar
2 envelopes unflavored gelatin
1 pt. cold milk
4 ozs. Cream of Coconut concentrate (available in a can—there are several Hawaiian and Puerto Rican brands)

5 drops almond extract
1 tsp. plum brandy (or other fruit liqueur)
Grated coconut, fresh raspberries, Mandarin oranges for garnish

NIGHT BEFORE:

◄§ RASPBERRY HALF

1. Simmer berries, sugar, and 1 cup water in heavy enameled saucepan, stirring occasionally.
2. When berries are shapeless and liquid is smooth, strain through very fine mesh sieve (or through standard sieve lined with 3 thicknesses of cheesecloth).
3. Cool liquid in refrigerator. (You can put in freezer, but do not allow to freeze.)

4. When cool, add 1 envelope gelatin powder and stir until completely dissolved.
5. Heat almost to boiling point to melt gelatin.
6. Half-fill 1-qt. round mold. Refrigerate. This must jell firmly before adding coconut half.

⋙ *COCONUT HALF*

1. Dissolve 1 envelope gelatin into milk, stirring until all grains disappear. (You may use hand beater.)
2. Place milk in enameled saucepan. Add coconut concentrate. Heat almost to boiling point, stirring occasionally. Add almond extract and plum brandy.
3. Refrigerate or put in freezer to chill. Stir occasionally while chilling to prevent coconut oil from rising to top. Do not allow to jell.
4. When cold, pour carefully into mold over firm berry gelatin.
5. Refrigerate overnight, covering mold with waxed paper or plastic wrap.

JUST BEFORE SERVING:

1. Immerse mold in shallow pan of hot (not boiling) water about 15 seconds. Do not allow water to get into gelatin.
2. Place serving platter upside-down over mold. Quickly flip over, remove mold. If necessary, tap mold sharply with wooden spoon to dislodge gelatin.
3. Garnish platter with fresh raspberries and grated coconut— also mandarin oranges if you wish.

NOTE: Blackberries, cranberries, or boysenberries may be substituted for raspberries.

SERVES 6.

TANGERINE MOUSSE WITH TANGERINE SYRUP

2 envelopes unflavored gelatin
2 cups hot fresh tangerine juice
  (approximately 8 tangerines)
3 eggs
2 egg yolks
Thinly sliced rind of ½ tangerine

3 tbsp. plus 1 cup granulated
  sugar
1 cup crushed ice
4 tangerines, peeled, sectioned,
  and seeded
½ cup shredded coconut

NIGHT BEFORE:

1. Pour gelatin and 1 cup tangerine juice into blender. Cover and blend at high speed 40 seconds.
2. Add eggs, yolks, rind, and 3 tbsp. sugar. Cover and blend at high speed 5 seconds.
3. Remove cover and, with motor on, add crushed ice. Blend 10 seconds.
4. Pour into 4-cup mold or individual molds.
5. Refrigerate overnight.
6. Make syrup of 1 cup tangerine juice and 1 cup sugar by bringing to boil quickly.
7. Refrigerate until serving time. When syrup is cool add sections of 1 tangerine.

JUST BEFORE SERVING:

1. Lower mold gently into shallow pan of hot (not boiling) water. Place serving platter upside down and reverse quickly. Tap bottom of mold with wooden spoon if necessary.
2. Garnish with sections of 3 tangerines and shredded coconut.
3. Serve topped with chilled tangerine syrup.

S E R V E S 6 .

ZABAGLIONE

6 egg yolks
2 eggs, whole
½ cup granulated sugar
½ cup Marsala wine
½ cup brandy
¼ tsp. cinnamon

½ tsp. vanilla extract
Bittersweet chocolate (for shavings for garnish)
1 cup heavy cream whipped (optional)
Maraschino cherries (optional)

NIGHT BEFORE:

1. In the top of 2-qt. double boiler, beat egg yolks and whole eggs with rotary beater 3 minutes.
2. Add sugar, beating in slowly.
3. Slowly beat in Marsala, brandy, cinnamon, and vanilla.
4. Boil water in bottom of double boiler. Add top and beat mixture with rotary beater or wire whisk 3–4 minutes, until mixture foams almost to top of pan. Do not overcook.
5. Remove from heat. Continue stirring with a spoon, scraping thickest part into rest, until mixture is smooth.
6. Pour into stem glasses or coffee cups.
7. Refrigerate overnight.

JUST BEFORE SERVING:

Serve cold, garnished with chocolate shavings, a spoonful of whipped cream with a cherry.

SERVES 8.

XII

BEVERAGES

XII

CRANBERRY-CASSIS PUNCH

1 cup French Sirop de Cassis
(black currant syrup)
3 glasses cranberry juice (measure
with glass the size you plan to
serve in, but ¾ full)

½ cup lemon juice
½ cup orange juice
2 glasses ginger ale (ditto above)

NIGHT BEFORE:
1. Mix all ingredients except ginger ale in a tall pitcher.
2. Refrigerate overnight.

JUST BEFORE SERVING:
1. Stir the mixture well, and add ginger ale.
2. Fill pitcher with ice cubes, and serve.

MAKES 6 GLASSES.

FANCY ICED COFFEE

6 cups double-strength coffee
8 tbsp. sugar
½ cup heavy cream

2 tbsp. cognac
Crushed ice

NIGHT BEFORE:
1. Prepare double-strength coffee. Refrigerate overnight.
2. Place 6 glasses filled with crushed ice in freezer overnight.

JUST BEFORE SERVING:
1. Mix coffee, sugar, cream, and cognac.

2. Pour half mixture into blender jar and blend about 15 seconds at high speed. Repeat with rest of coffee.
3. Take glasses out of freezer at last minute, pour freshly blended coffee over crushed ice, and serve with straws. The outside of the glasses should be well frosted by the time you get to the table.

MAKES 6 GLASSES.

GLOGG
Scandinavian Hot Spiced Wine Punch

Ideal for wintry evenings and Christmas entertaining, this colorful punch is most attractive served in glass punch cups. Its flavor is rich and lusty—a serious and delicious drink.

10 cardamom pods	1 cup toasted blanched almonds
12 cloves	1 cup white raisins
1 2" cinnamon stick	Rind of ½ orange
1 bottle claret	½ lb. cube sugar
1 bottle port	1 pt. cognac
	½ orange, thinly sliced

NIGHT BEFORE.

1. Tie cardamom pods, cloves, and cinnamon stick in square of cheesecloth.
2. Pour claret and port into heavy saucepan. Add tied spices. Add almonds, raisins, and orange rind.
3. Heat mixture to boiling point. Remove from heat, discard orange rind, and refrigerate overnight.

JUST BEFORE SERVING:

1. Reheat wine mixture until barely simmering but not boiling.
2. In separate saucepan, melt sugar cubes in cognac over low heat. Pour this mixture into wine mixture.
3. Transfer mixture to punch bowl and float orange slices on top.
4. Serve with a few almonds and raisins in each cup.

MAKES 24 PUNCH CUPS.

HOT OR ICED CHOCOLATE DRINK

6 tbsp. best Dutch cocoa   *4 tbsp. granulated sugar*
1½ qts. milk (you may use   *(or more, to taste)*
*   skimmed milk)*   *1 tsp. grated nutmeg*

NIGHT BEFORE:

1. In heavy enameled saucepan, bring ½ cup water to simmer.
2. While it is heating, measure out cocoa and have it ready at hand.
3. When water simmers, toss in cocoa quickly, and with a wooden spoon stir vigorously until a thick, pasty syrup is formed and all the little dry lumps of cocoa are dissolved.
4. Keep flame at medium-low. Now add milk, about ½ cup at a time, stirring frequently until all milk is added, but do not allow to boil.
5. Add sugar (to taste) and nutmeg.
6. Remove from heat and refrigerate, covered, overnight.

JUST BEFORE SERVING:

Hot: Reheat over medium-low flame just short of boiling point. Strain and serve.

Cold: Strain and serve over crushed ice in glasses.

MAKES 6 CUPS.

SPICED HONEY TEA

6 *Orange Pekoe tea bags*   1 *stick cinnamon*
6 *tbsp. orange blossom honey (or*   ½ *cup fresh lemon juice*
other clear, liquid honey, not
the white, crystallized type)

NIGHT BEFORE:

1. Steep tea bags in 6 cups boiling water until a dark tea results.
2. Remove bags, and turn on low flame. Add honey and stir thoroughly.
3. Add cinnamon stick and lemon juice. Allow to simmer 5 minutes.
4. Remove from heat and refrigerate overnight.

JUST BEFORE SERVING:

Hot: Reheat to boil, remove cinnamon stick, and serve.

Iced: Reheat to boil, remove cinnamon stick, and pour over ice in tall glasses.

NOTE: For iced tea, it is always best to use ice cubes made from tea in advance, thus maintaining the strength of the iced tea.

MAKES 6 CUPS.

TANGY PINEAPPLE-GRAPEFRUIT COCKTAIL

3 *cups grapefruit juice (fresh is*   1 *cup lime juice*
best, but canned if necessary)   ⅔ *cup granulated sugar*
1½ *cups pineapple juice (frozen*   Mint
or canned)

NIGHT BEFORE:

1. Boil sugar and ⅔ cup water 3 minutes. Refrigerate overnight.
2. If using canned grapefruit juice, blend with pineapple and lime juices and sugar-water syrup in blender. Refrigerate overnight.
3. Put glasses in freezer to ice them.

JUST BEFORE SERVING:

1. If using fresh grapefruit juice, blend with pineapple and lime juices and sugar-water syrup in a blender.
2. Pour into frozen glasses. Garnish with mint. Serve immediately.

MAKES 6 CUPS.

VEGETABLE-CLAM JUICE COCKTAIL

3 cups V-8 juice
3 cups clam juice
¼ cup fresh lemon juice
¼ tsp. Worcestershire sauce

⅛ tsp. salt
⅛ tsp. white pepper
6 slim raw carrot sticks (for use as stirrers)

NIGHT BEFORE:

Combine all ingredients except carrot sticks in a pitcher, mix well, and refrigerate overnight.

JUST BEFORE SERVING:

Run mixture through blender and serve in iced glasses with carrot sticks as first course.

NOTE: This can be the basis of an unusual "Clam Bloody Mary" by the addition of vodka.

SERVES 6.

XIII

TWENTY SUGGESTED MENUS

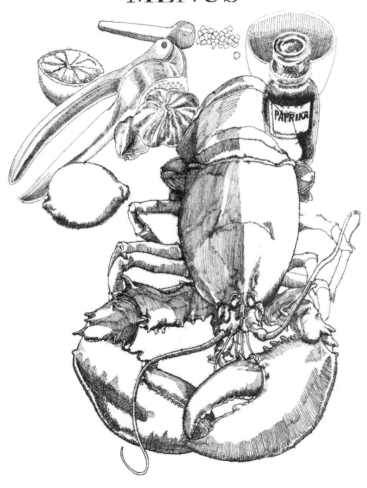

XIII

These twenty menus are offered only as suggestions, with some discussion of appropriate wines, and should not be treated as requirements. Although they do offer the possibility of preparing entire meals the night before, substitutions can easily be made.

We have tried to make balanced menus and provide some contrasts of taste and temperature. We have suggested two wines when two different courses in one menu seemed to require it. You'll find one Oriental menu, some rather simple, hearty ones, and others intended for more elaborate entertaining, such as the menu featuring Chinese Roast Pork, which cries out for the best wines. Also you'll find that some of the lighter menus are better for the warmer months, while others are intended for the coldest weather.

The wine suggestions are written with the intention of giving you some latitude of choice, and we have tried to avoid naming just one expensive wine that might be hard to find *and* pay for! You'll also notice that in one menu a suggestion of beer or ale crept in.

An extra tip on using these suggested menus: If you plan to really do the entire menu the night before, make sure you have enough refrigerator space and storage containers for the recipes in the one you choose. Otherwise you might find yourself staring at a melting dessert or hardening sauce and nowhere to put it!

Chinese Ch'un Chuan Spring Rolls with Plum Sauce
Egg Flower Soup   Oriental Beef with Oyster Sauce
Chinese Fried Rice   Sweet-and-Sour Salad
Mandarin Orange Chiffon Pie

A white Graves, 1961, 1962, or 1964. Beef ordinarily would call for a red wine, but because of the character of this oriental food, a semisweet wine like the Graves is better.

Avocado-Stuffed Tomatoes　　　Potage St. Germain
Marinated Broiled Lamb Chops
Duchess Potatoes　　　Lettuce Salad with Roquefort Dressing
Crème Brulee

St. Julien, 1955, 1959, 1961, or 1962. Ideal: Chateau Leoville Poyferré or Chateau Leoville Lascases.

Clams Casino　　　Madrilene Surprise
Lobster in Sherry Cream Sauce
Hagymas Paprikas Krumpli (Boiled Paprika Potatoes)
Cucumber Cream Salad
Bombe Rothschild

A moselle, Spätlese class, 1964. Example: Ockfener Bockstein Spätlese or (rather expensive) Bernkasteler Doktor Spätlese.

Sashimi　　　Cheese Soup
Boiled Beef with Horseradish Currant Sauce
Mushroom Salad
Pecan Torte Wanda

A Rosé. A 1964 Anjou would be best.

Greek Lemon Soup
Chicken Cotelettes Polonaise with Dill Sauce
Stuffed Baked Tomatoes　　　Salade Russe
Canton Fruit Cup

A regional white Burgundy, such as Puligny Montrachet or Pouilly Fuissé.

Fresh Lobster Pâté   Bongo Bongo Soup
Marinade de Boeuf Naomi
Carrot Pudding
Potato Salad in Sour Cream Dressing
Linzer Tészta
With the lobster: A Meursault (white Burgundy) 1961 or 1964.
With the beef: A Chambertin, a Clos Vougeot, or an estates bottled
Nuits St. George. All 1955 or 1959.

Pelmeny Siberian
Japanese Tempura Shrimps
Quick Fried Rice   Salade Espagñole
Cranberry Kissel
A Chablis, 1961 or 1964. Or a less expensive substitute, a Sancerre
1961 or 1964. Also possible: an Alsatian or German Gewürtz-
traminer, 1961, 1962, or 1964.

Quiche Lorraine
Broiled Chicken
Night Before Fruit and Mint Salad
Pots de Crème au Chocolat
A white Burgundy. In the expensive class: Montrachet, Chevalier
Montrachet, or Batârd Montrachet, 1961 or 1964. Less expensive:
a regional Puligny-Montrachet. A light red wine would also be
acceptable.

Cold Avocado Soup
Hungarian Veal and Mushroom Rolls
Hagymas Paprikas Krumpli (Boiled Paprika Potatoes)
Eggplant Salad
Csokolade Torta
A light red Burgundy. An estate-bottled Beaune or Volnay 1959,
1961, 1962, or 1964.

Chicken Liver Pâté
Jambalaya   Steamed Rice
Crabmeat and Bean Sprout Salad
Babka au Rhum
A 1961 or 1964 Chablis.

Rolled Sandwich Hors d'Oeuvres
Beef Stroganoff
Steamed Rice   Salade Russe
Frozen Bavarian Cream with Cranberry-Orange Sauce
This menu really should be complemented by a very good wine.
Serve the best Bordeaux in the house, such as a Chateau Margaux
or Chateau Haut Brion, or any other good wine from the Margaux,
Graves, or St. Julien districts of Bordeaux. Years: 1945, 1949,
1953, 1955, or 1959.

Curried Beef Hors d'Oeuvres   Artichoke Soup
Coq au Vin
Duchess Potatoes   Lettuce with Lemon Salad Dressing
Crème Renversée au Caramel
A light red Burgundy, 1959, 1961, or 1962. Also a white Burgundy
would be appropriate, such as a Meursault 1961 or 1964.

Off-Beat Borscht
Spareribs and Sauerkraut Casserole   Garlic Bread
Potato Salad in Sour Cream Dressing
Almond Blancmange
A white Traminer or Sylvaner from Alsace, 1959, 1961, or 1964.
Also very appropriate: beer or ale.

Gazpacho
Roast Stuffed Squab
Creamed Spinach Ring with Sherry
Baked Glazed Yams   Red Cabbage Salad
Tangerine Mousse with Tangerine Syrup

A good Bordeaux is appropriate here. Or, a good white Graves
would also do, 1961, 1962, or 1964.

Striped Bass in Aspic with Sauce Verte
Tournedos with Fois Gras
String Beans à la Française   Scalloped Potatoes au Gratin
Mousse au Chocolat

With the striped bass: A good Meursault (Perrières if available)
1961 or 1964, or a Corton Charlemagne of the same vintages.
With the tournedos: An important Bordeaux such as Chateau
Latour, Chateau Lafite, Chateau Mouton, Chateau Lynch Bages,
or other wine from the Pauillac district. Vintages: 1953 or older
for the first three, and 1955 or 1959 for the rest.

Hot Vichyssoise   Scandinavian Salad
Veal Steaks in Sour Cream
Cauliflower and Broccoli Pie
Rouge et Blanc Suprême

A light Burgundy: Beaune, Volnay, Savigny, or Santenay, 1959,
1961, or 1962. An interesting alternative: a Rhone wine, Cote
Rotie, same vintages as the Burgundy.

Rumaki   Connoisseur's Mushroom Soup
Chinese Roast Pork
Beets Nela   Chinese Fried Rice
Lettuce Salad with Green Goddess Dressing
Apricot Mousse

Several choices here: A Tavel Rosé, a semisweet Anjou, or a
white Graves or Vouvray. Vintages for all should be 1961 or 1964.

Iced Tomato Soup
Marinated Filets of Beef
Baked Eggplant   German Bean Salad
Cheese Pie

A Rhone wine. A red Hermitage or Chateauneuf du Pape 1955, 1959, or 1961. Alternative: an important Beaujolais such as Moulin à Vent 1964.

Oeufs en Gelée with Crabmeat
Broiled Shrimps   Mushrooms Florentine
Coeurs à la Crême

With the eggs: A white Burgundy such as Pouilly Fuissé or regional Puligny-Montrachet 1964.
With the shrimps: an estate-bottled Montrachet or Corton Charlemagne or a white Clos de Vougeot 1961 or 1964.

Cold Poached Trout
Lemon Chicken   Steamed Rice
Green Salad with French Garlic Dressing
Apple Sauce   Almond Sugar Sticks

With the trout: A Moselle 1964, preferable but not necessarily estate-bottled.
With the chicken: A great Rhine wine of the Spätlese or Auslese class, a Schloss Vollrads, a Marcobrunner, or a Forster 1959 or 1964.
Here the salad must be served after the second wine, because of the garlic.

INDEX

INDEX

Almond
    blancmange, 168-169
    -cucumber salad dressing, 142
    frosting, 152-153
    sugar sticks, 148
Anchovy pie, Norwegian, 92
Appetizers
    Camembert cheese dip, 9
    chick pea spread (or dip), 12-13
    clams Casino, 12
    curried beef, 13
    gnocchi tidbits, 15-16
    ham and cream cheese balls, 15
    Japanese raw fish, 21-22
    pâté
        chicken liver, 9-10
        lobster, 14
    pickled onions, 16
    Polynesian rumaki, 20-21
    quiche Lorraine, 17-19
    rolled sandwich, 19-20
    spring rolls with plum sauce, 10-11
    stuffed soft rolls, 22
    tomatoes stuffed with avocado, 8
    See also Hors d'oeuvres
Apple
    sauce, 169
    Swiss roll, 164-165
Appliances, 2-4
Apricot mousse, 169-170
Arroz con bananas, 65-66
Artichoke soup, 28-29
Aspic
    eggs with crabmeat in, 104-105
    ham in, 53-54
    striped bass in, 98-99
Avocado
    -chicken salad, 132
    cream dessert, 175

Avocado, *Continued*
    soup, 24
    tomatoes stuffed with, 8

Babka au rhum, 149
Bacon and cheese filling, 17-18
Baghdad meat-fruit casserole, 49
Baked desserts, *see* Desserts
Bananas
    raisin cake loaf with, 161
    rice and leftover meat with, 65-66
Bass in aspic, 98-99
Bavarian cream with cranberry-orange sauce, 177-178
Bean sprout and crabmeat salad, 133
Beans
    à la française, 124
    German salad, 136
Beef
    arroz con bananas, 65-66
    bleu cheese burgers, 41
    boiled with horseradish currant sauce, 42
    chili con carne, 43
    curried hors d'oeuvres, 12
    filets of, marinated, 46-47
    and fruit casserole, 49
    Hungarian stuffed cabbage with, 68-69
    Irish potato pie, 44-45
    marinade de Naomi, 45-46
    in meat loaf, 67
    'n ale casserole, 38-39
    oriental, with oyster sauce, 47
    rice and bananas with, 65-66
    sauerbraten, 48
    Sikbaj, 49
    Spanish meat balls, 68
    Stroganoff, 39-40

202